AF522353

National Human Rights Commission

Sankar Sen

First Published 2018

ISBN 978-93-83723-17-1

Published by
LG PUBLISHERS DISTRIBUTORS
49, Street No. 14, Pratap Nagar,
Mayur Vihar Phase I, Delhi 110091
Email: lgpdist@gmail.com

Designed by
Limited Colors, Delhi 110 092

Printed at
Sapra Brothers, Delhi 110 092

Contents

Justice Shivaraj V. Patil

Formerly Judge,
High Court of Karnataka,
High Court of Madras,
Chief Justice, High Court of Rajasthan,
Supreme Court of India and
Member, National Human Rights Commission

"Sparsh",
254, 18th Cross,
Sadashivanagar,
Bangalore-560 080
Ph. : +91-80-2361 0334, 2361 6644
e-mail : jsvp1940@gmail.com

FOREWORD

I am delighted, rather privileged to write the Foreword to this book titled "National Human Rights Commission" by Mr. Sankar Sen. He was a distinguished member of Indian Police Service from Odisha cadre. He served in different positions efficiently and effectively while in service. As the Director of Sardar Vallabhbhai Patel National Police Academy, he brought many meaningful, useful and innovative changes in the training programmes of Indian Police. He served as the first Director General (DG) of National Human Rights Commission (NHRC) and was instrumental in building up an excellent Police Wing. He was awarded the Police Medal for Distinguished Service in 1986. A large number of his articles on Law Enforcement, Terrorism, Human Rights and Trafficking, etc., have appeared in national dailies and well-known magazines in and outside the Country. Presently, he is serving as Senior Fellow at the Institute of Social Sciences, New Delhi. After retirement from public service, he is usefully and not necessary gainfully engaged in serving the society. *He is no more a public servant but he is ever in public service.*

When I was in NHRC as a member between 2005 to 2008, he interacted with me on many occasions on various issues touching Human Rights violations, about reforms and steps to be taken to make Human Rights meaningful more particularly, for those vulnerable sections in the society, be they women, children, persons in custody, sick and suffering, less fortunate and voiceless. I was impressed by his passion for Human Rights and his undying sprit to serve the cause of promotion and protection of Human Rights. This book in my view, is a great value addition to the literature on Human Rights, the focus being on NHRC. The author having been a part of NHRC in a responsible position has done justice to the subject. This book reflects his hard work, dedication, commitment, concern, respect for human rights and knowledge. In my opinion, a book written with insight and practical experience gained on the ground relating to the subject, will be more meaningful and effective in serving the aims, objects and purposes for which it is written, besides creating deeper impact on a reader.

The book is appropriately designed, containing precise narration of facts, critical analysis of issues, references to relevant statutory provisions, international instruments and conventions, functionality and working experience of NHRC and valuable suggestions for reforms and improvements in working of the Commission. Undoubtedly the glory and greatness; quality and utility; relevance and reverence of any democratic institution, depend on the integrity, functional efficiency and commitment of the persons associated with it. *In my opinion, the chair being the same, the occupant can make tremendous difference by his performance in any organization.* The foundation, the structure, interiors, living and functioning of NHRC are mirrored well by the Architect Mr. Sankar Sen in the book, right from genesis to evaluation. The book is spread over in 15 Chapters.

Mr. Sankar Sen in his book has traced the facts, the events and the circumstances leading to enacting to the protection of Human Rights Act, 1993. The Act, provides for establishment of the National Human Rights Commission and State Human Rights Commissions. It provides a broad mandate to the Commission. The Commission has a jurisdiction to enquire into petitions concerning "violation of Human Rights or abetment thereof or negligence in the prevention of violation by a public servant". The process of selection of Chairman and Members, its composition and statutory positions indicate the status, credibility and functional autonomy of the Commission although there is no full financial autonomy.

He recollects that the announcement of the formation of NHRC evoked mixed reactions. Some felt that the Commission would be a Toothless Tiger; may function as a post Office and in fact it would be only "A Sarkari Commission". Over the years NHRC by its performance has shown that it may not have teeth but it has a strong denture to bite having regard to the composition, status and public opinion and further that the report of the Commission has to be placed before the Parliament annually. In case concerned government/authorities did not take action as recommended by the Commission, opposition parties will point out the same. Further the strong public opinion is another factor to compel the authorities to act on the basis of the recommendations of the Commission. I understand mostly recommendations of the Commission are accepted by the Government and complied with.

The author has written about evolution and crystallization of National Human Rights Institutions (NHRIs). United Nations (UN) had considered the subject of NHRI even as early as in 1946 before adoption of the Universal Declaration of Human Rights. In the year 1991 the UN Committee on Human Rights had called a conference to study the entire issue. The workshop held in Paris devised principles relating to the status of the National institutions. These principles are popularly known as "Paris Principles". In the world conference on Human Rights in 1993 convened in Vienna reaffirmed the important and constructive role to be played by the national institutions, for promotion and protection of Human Rights.

Mr. Sen speaks of early years in the journey of NHRC. He has taken pains to narrate problems and deficiencies faced in its working. It is also stated that the efforts were made to establish proper wings including the investigation wing. The author had major role in structuring of investigation wing in the beginning. In any institution/organization the framework and functional structure built by the persons at the initial stage of establishment will have better impact in terms of serving the real purpose for which a public institution is established and exists.

He states that having had the working experience for few years, the Commission felt the necessity of reviewing the protection of Human Rights Act and to suggest amendments in order to make functions of the Commission more effective. A Committee was set up for the purpose.

The author talks about the status of the Human Rights Commission and about armed forces and jurisdiction of the Human Rights Commission. A detailed discussion is made on the police and prison reforms and about the significant contribution made by the Commission in that regard.

The issue of bonded labour is dealt with in the book. It is unfortunate, yet a fact that despite statutory provisions, the reprehensible bonded labour system in some or the other form is still prevailing in the country. The author refers to various statutory provisions relating to the issue, magnitude of the problem and the initiatives taken by the NHRC. Similar issues, problems and remedies are considered by the author on child labour and child marriage as well.

Handling of complaints by the Commission and its mechanism, is captured in the book. One of the substantial functions of the Commission is to enquire into the complaints of Human Rights violations by public servants through their acts of commission, omission and negligence. The complaints handling mechanism of the Commission and the functioning of the investigation wing need to be credited. The personnel of the Commission were invited to few other countries for training their personnel in complaint handling mechanism. Facts and figures are also given relating to nature of complaints, custodial death cases, custodial violations, etc., in the book

Human Rights education is another topic dealt with in the book. The preamble of the Universal Declaration of Human Rights, 1948 (UDHR) clearly states that recognition and respect for human rights is a foundation of freedom, peace and justice in the Country. Article 26(2) of the UDHR declares that, *"Education shall be directed to the full development of a human personality and to the strengthening of respect of human rights and fundamental freedoms. It shall promote understanding, tolerance and friendship among the nations, racial or religious groups and shall further the activities of the United Nations for the maintenance of peace"*. The author says that only when people become aware of their rights they will be able to assert and enforce their rights. *It may be added here that creating awareness among people about the Human Rights is important but it is equally important to sensitize the field functionaries about the impact and importance of Human Rights.*

Review of laws and international instruments on Human Rights and Human Rights issues relating to vulnerable groups are elaborately stated in the book referring to the problems, relevant legislations and NHRC interventions. Suggestions are also made to improve/reform the position. Social and economic rights are considered referring to Article 25*(1) of UDHR, the International covenant on Economic, Social and Cultural Rights (1996) and Article 21 of the Constitution of India. Reference is made to Food Security Bill and Right to Health in the book.

In conclusion, the author has made evaluation of the work of NHRC, right from its inception. He concludes that in the ultimate analysis "Human Rights in a developing country like India have a transformative potential. They constitute challenges to the entrenched interests and provide tools for building a just and humane society. The NHRC in its chequered annals of more than two decades have been able to right many wrongs done to individuals and wipe the tears from some eyes. But, it has encountered stubborn resistance from entrenched interests as well as from authorities while trying to bring about systemic changes".

I am of the view that there is a need for concerted, cooperative and collective efforts by different sections of the society in the matter of protection and promotion of Human Rights. *In that the ever vigilant civil society, dedicated NGOs, honest and committed law enforcing agencies, pro-active judiciary and positive meaningful and purposive media have to work towards the same goal of respecting Human Rights to achieve and accomplish the aims and objects envisaged in the protection of Human Rights Act 1993.*

This book is the result of hard work, dedication, commitment, experience and knowledge of Mr. Sankar Sen. I have good reasons to think that all the stakeholders in the field, students, teachers and the citizens interested in and concerned with respect for Human Rights, will be immensely benefitted by reading this book. My best wishes to the author to continue to produce more such quality products in the form of books for the consumption of the evolving, developing and transforming society.

(Justice Shivaraj V. Patil)

1
Genesis

Till the early 1990s the Government of India did not pay adequate attention to human rights issues and concerns. Reports and petitions on human rights abuses in anti-terrorist and anti-insurgency operations in Jammu and Kashmir and North-Eastern states were not taken seriously. Often they met with deafening silence. But serious criticisms of human rights violations were levelled by civil rights activists and also from international organizations like Amnesty International and Asia Watch. In their reports they accused the Government of India of condoning human rights abuses and providing immunity to the security forces. These international groups in 1991-92 levelled criticisms on the basis of fact-finding missions.

In the US Congress human rights violations by the security forces in Punjab and Kashmir were the focus of a debate in 1990-91 sparked off by introduction of a measure calling for cutting off all US development aid if the Indian government did not allow human rights groups access to India. The Bill sponsored by Dan Burton was aimed at gaining access for Amnesty International which had been barred from conducting fact finding missions. An amended version of the Bill was adopted by the House without the aid cut off[1].

Speaking on March 16, 1992, the then Home Minister S.B. Chavan told the Rajya Sabha that "the purpose of the proposed human rights commission was to counter false and politically motivated propaganda by foreign and Indian civil rights agencies[2].

On April 24, 1992, Mr. V.N. Gadgil the official spokesperson of the Congress Party, stated that his party would call for a national consensus on the role and the powers of a proposed National Human Rights Commission. The commission's findings, according to him would act as "corrective to the biased and one-sided reports of the NGOs and also be an effective answer to politically motivated international criticism[3].

Important precedents already existed for doing so. India's Parliament had already created two related commissions—a National Commission for Scheduled Castes and Scheduled Tribes in 1990 and a National Commission for Minorities in 1992—an approach for setting up of the commission. The meeting examined the possibility of placing constitutional civil liberties within the ambit of the Commission as well as enacting legislation on custodial deaths. A Committee under the Chairmanship of the Home Minister was set up to look into the proposal. At the instance of the committee it was decided to have wide-ranging discussions on the subject with eminent persons representing a cross section of the society such as jurists, lawyers, journalists, academicians, administrators and other public personalities. Four seminars one each in Mumbai, Kolkata, Delhi and Hyderabad were organized through the concerned state governments. The Home Minister had detailed discussions with the Chief Secretaries and Directors General of Police of the State Government. After this elaborate exercise the Human Rights Bill 1993 was prepared and introduced in the Lok Sabha on May 14, 1993.

On May 14, 1993, the Government of India introduced the Human Rights Bill, 1993.999 (Bill No. 65, 1993). Instead of following the accepted practice of first referring the bill to the Parliamentary Standing Committee for scrutiny, the Home Minister first introduced the bill in the Parliament and then referred the bill to the Parliamentary Standing Committee[4].

The original bill envisaged a bureaucratic composition of the commission. It provided that the Commission will have four members besides the Chairman. It stipulated that out of four members, one must have experience in general administration at the level of Secretary to the Government of India or an equivalent post (b) at the level of Secretary or equivalent post, at legal affairs or an equivalent post of judge of High Court or a distinguished jurist. (c) Experience in police administration at the level of Secretary to the Government of India or equivalent post.

This proposal of the composition of the commission evoked sharp criticisms from different quarters. Many members of Parliament as well as different NGO groups expressed apprehensions that this kind of bureaucratic composition would adversely impact on the credibility of the commission. It would be looked upon as a body somewhat over-weighted in favour of people with official and bureaucratic background and thus would lack credibility. In the light of the criticisms made regarding the original bill an ordinance was first passed by the government creating the Commission. Another bill was presented in the Parliament on November 25, 1993 to replace the ordinance. The bill received Presidential assent on January 8, 1994.

Responding to the criticisms of the bureaucratic composition of the Commission envisaged earlier, the then Home Minster during discussion on the bill in the Parliament said that though the government had good reasons to provide for an element of administrative experience in the commission, but in view of the feeling that such a provision would affect the credibility of the commission, the government had modified the provision and now the majority of the persons would be members from the judicial background. He further said that "the Commission has not been conceived as a stand-alone institution, but a body through its multiple functions including enquiry into specific cases can bring about awareness of human rights promotion, enforcement of the existing safeguards and bring greater accountability to the system".

A Standing Committee of the Parliament heard the views of jurists, academics and important public personalities. The well-known jurist, Soli Sorabjee, in his evidence tendered before the Committee said, that two important things are to be kept in mind: first, the credibility of the Commission and second its effectiveness. He expressed unhappiness that the functions of the Commission are recommendatory and hortatory. It can merely make recommendations to the government for prosecution of errant officials or grant of relief. It has no powers to punish the violation of human rights. Of course, it can be a supplicatory litigant before the Supreme Court or the High Courts and pray for directions and orders. That is what public-spirited NGOs have been doing for years. He added that "exclusion of the military and security forces from the scrutiny of the commission is the first act of its emasculation". He observed that a provision may be made for co-opting in the Commission a high ranking army officer when it is dealing with complaints against the armed forces.

Another jurist, Justice Rajendra Sachar, former Chief Justice of Delhi High Court, said, that clause 14 of the Bill has a serious defect. It does not give the commission its own staff. The commission for the purpose of conducting any investigation has to use the services of officers of any investigating agency with the concurrence of the central or state government. He felt that the human rights commission should not be a wing of the CBI or Vigilance Commission. It is an independent body and would not be dependent on others for its staff requirements. During discussions in the Parliament another member Syed Sahabuddin questioned the motive of the government in bringing forward this bill. He said that the government perhaps introduced this bill "out of strategic compulsions of our economic relations". He also criticized the exclusion of the security forces from the purview of the commission more or less. According to him "the term "armed forces" has been defined in a very comprehensive manner and since most of the violations that had been reported are acts committed by the armed forces the commission should have the authority to go into their acts[5].

Replying to the discussions in the Parliament the then Home Minister S.B. Chavan said, "let me say with all the force at my command that it was not because of pressures exerted by any party or any country that we have brought this bill. But I cannot remain oblivious of the fact that there are certain countries which are very interested in maligning the image of India and they are going to take full advantage of the UN Assembly and that was exactly the reason we thought that before hearing the criticisms before the UN Assembly and thereafter bringing this bill would have created a different kind of atmosphere". Further, responding to the criticisms that the Commission's powers are recommendatory and it will function as a toothless tiger, the Home Minister said that "we have a Finance Commission which is a recommendatory body, the government has the right to reject its recommendations but it never does so". The National Human Rights Commission, according to him, is a high-powered body presided over by the retired Chief Justice of the Supreme Court and two of the judges of the Supreme Court and High Court. These are the people who constitute the commission and that is why we have to create the necessary atmosphere. The government does not have a restrictive attitude towards them.

The statement of Objects and Reasons of the Bill made clear the purpose of the act which was subsequently adopted. While noting that India was a party to the International Covenant on Civil and Political Rights and Covenant on Economic and Social and Cultural Rights, and rights embodied in those covenants are substantially protected by the Constitution of India, the statement observed that "there had been a growing concern in the country relating to human rights. Having regard to this and to changing realities and emerging trends in the nature of crime and violence, it had been considered essential to review the existing procedures and laws and the system of administration with a view to bringing greater efficiency and transparency."

There has been justifiable criticism of the government for not consulting human rights activists and other civil society groups closely associated with human rights. There was a limited number of government consultations. The government's "Background Note on Setting Up of a National Commission of Human Rights – Issues and Tentative Framework" was not released to the public nor was it placed before the Parliament. It is true that India has long sought international solutions to its human rights problems, but in the absence of international pressures, norms and cooperation it is unlikely that India would have created a National Human Rights Commission per se. (Charles Norchi, supra note 5, Despite the claim of the government to the contrary, many social activists viewed

NHRC as internationally inspired. Ravi Nayar, Executive Director SAHRDC went to the extent of describing it as an effort to "circumvent international scrutiny by stating that they have adequate national institutions to investigate these charges (Ravi Nayar-*New York Times* cited in Norchi, The National Human Rights Commission of India".

Composition of NHRC

The Protection of the Human Rights Act, 1993, provides for establishment of the National Human Rights Commission and State Human Rights Commissions. Section 3 of the Act provides for constitution of a Commission consisting of (a) a Chairperson who has been the Chief Justice of the Supreme Court (b) a Member who has been a judge of the Supreme Court (c) one Member who has been a judge of the High Court (d) one Member to be appointed from amongst persons with knowledge of and practical experience in matters relating to human rights. Section 4 of the Act lays down a new and confidence -inspiring procedure for the selection of the Chairman and the other members. It laid down that the Chairman and other members of the Commission shall be appointed by the President of India on the recommendations of a Committee consisting of (a) the Prime Minister, (b) Speaker of the Lok Sabha, (c) Deputy Chairman of the Rajya Sabha (d) Minister-in-charge of Home Affairs (e) Leader of the Opposition in the Lok Sabha and (f) Leader of the opposition—Rajya Sabha. Section 5 of the Act provides that the Chairman or any Member of the Commission can be removed from office on grounds of "proven misbehaviour" only after an enquiry by the Supreme Court after a reference to it to be made by the President. The Act further provides for two other important posts, viz. a Secretary General, an officer of the rank of the Secretary to the Government of India to function as the Chief Executive Officer of the Commission and an officer of the rank of the Director General of Police to head the Investigation Wing of the Commission.

The Human Rights Act provides a broad mandate to the Commission. The Commission has a jurisdiction to enquire into petitions concerning "violation of human rights or abetment thereof or negligence in the prevention of violation by a public servant[6].

(1) Among other powers, the Commission may intervene in any proceeding involving any allegation of violation of human rights pending before a court with the approval of such a court; (2) Visit any jail or any other institution under the control of the state government, where persons are detained or lodged for purposes of treatment, reformation or protection to study the living conditions of the inmates and make recommendations thereon; (3) Review the safeguards provided by the Constitution or any other law for the protection of human rights and recommend measures for their effective implementation; (4) Review the factors, including acts of terrorism, that inhibit the enjoyment of human rights; (5) Study treaties and other international instruments on human rights and make recommendations for their effective implementation; and (6) Undertake and promote research in the field of human rights.

This wide range of functions under the act confers on the Commission the entire range of powers contemplated by the Paris Principles. The National Commission has also been given the powers of a civil court trying a suit relating to summoning and enforcing of attendance of witnesses, discovery and production of any document, receiving evidence or affidavits, requisitioning any public record or copy thereof from any court or office[7]".

The NHRC does not however enjoy any substantial financial autonomy. Although it receives Parliament approved grants, the actual amount to be paid is decided by the government. Nonetheless, funding through parliament, as opposed to a particular ministry, has certain inbuilt checks because the opposition parties may thwart the government's attempt to starve the commission. Thus this method ensures a greater degree of financial autonomy for the Commission.

Announcement of the formation of the NHRC evoked mixed reactions. While many had an open and unbiased mind and wanted the Commission to shape up and fare well, a number of human rights activists held negative views and opinions. They felt that the statute was flawed and the Commission would be a toothless tiger and merely function as a post office. In reality, it would only be a "Sarkari Commission" and will seek to whitewash the omissions and commissions of the government. It would fail to ensure better protection of human rights which was the avowed intention of the Commission. Some even went to the extent of saying that the Commission would do a disservice to the human rights movement of the country and offer only placebos. The real challenge before the Commission was to disprove the Cassandras and demonstrate its effectiveness and credibility before the country.

Some NGOs like South Asia Human Rights Documentation Centre (SAHRDC)[8], have questioned the procedure of appointment of the chairperson and the members. It expressed the view that the "appointment committee is not free from political influence and in practice recommendations evince a pro-government bias". Of the six committee members including the Chairman, opposition leaders were granted only two seats because the Prime Minister, Lok Sabha speaker, Home Minister and the Deputy Chairman of the Rajya Sabha may all be the members of the ruling party and are able to form the majority. It suggests that a more equitable and responsible way to appoint the members is to confirm the nomination through parliamentary hearings. A committee could be empowered to gather information about the candidates from the public and from the representatives of the ruling and opposition parties. Such a process would ensure a better and more open deliberative process and in turn safeguard the independence and impartiality of the Commission.

Endnotes

1. *Human Rights Development 1991 Report,* State Department Annual Country Reports on Human Rights Practice.
2. John Cockel, *State Institutions and Human Rights in India.*
3. South Asia Human Rights Documentation Centre (SAHRDC), Human Rights Commission: Mirage or Oasis, discussion paper for the First all India Consultation of Human Rights Activists, September 1992.
4. Dissertation on National Human Rights Commission: A Human Rights Evaluation by Reenu Paul.
5. Discussions in Parliament on Protection of Human Rights Bill, December 18, 1993.
6. Section 12A, Human Rights Act 1993.
7. Section 13(1) of the Human Rights Act 1993.
8. Judgment Reserved—Case of National Human Rights Commission, p. 22.

2

National Human Rights Institutions

The subject of National Human Rights Institutions (NHRI) had been considered by the United Nations, albeit sporadically, since its founding. Even as early as 1946, two years before the adoption of the Universal Declaration of Human Rights (UDHR), the Economic and Social Council of United Nations (ECOSOS) was using the term national institutions in its discussions on human rights and urging member states to consider the desirability of establishing human rights groups and local human rights committees at the national level to collaborate with ECOSOS in furthering the work of the UN Commission on Human Rights.

However, there was little significant progress during the next 30 years. The cold war affected the evolution of human rights institutions and coloured the debate in the United Nations that hampered protection and promotion of human rights. ECOSOS did adopt a resolution in 1960 that acknowledged the importance of NHRIs in a more proactive way and stressed the unique role that a national institution can play in the promotion of human rights[1]. In 1978 the United Nations Commission on Human Rights organized a seminar on human rights in Geneva exclusively devoted to the role of national and social institutions for the promotion of human rights. The seminar approved a set of guidelines for the role as well as functioning of such institutions. The guidelines were subsequently endorsed by the Commission and the General Assembly[2]. These guidelines covered the types of promotional and advisory activities the national institutions should carry out and the institutional modalities involved. But the outcome of the initiatives of the United Nations was limited. Very few independent NHRIs had been established in any region.

Paris Principles

Against this backdrop, the UN Commission on Human Rights called a conference in 1991 with the participation of national and regional institutions to study the entire issue. The workshop held in Paris devised principles relating to the status of national institutions. These principles came to be known as Paris Principles.

The Paris Principles are not legally binding international rules. Although the workshop that drafted and adopted the Principles was convened in response to the request of the UN Commission on Human Rights, the standards originally only represented the views of a handful of national institutions, NGOs and a limited number of state governments. With time, however, the Principles have gained widespread acceptance and acquired considerable political and moral weight.

The Paris Principles articulate the status and responsibilities of NHRIs and lay down the normative framework of the NHRIs. Subsequently they were also endorsed by the General Assembly[3].

The Paris Principles are the first systematic effort to enumerate the functions of NHRIs. They are divided into sections comprising certain headings—competence and responsibilities, composition and guarantees of independence and pluralism, methods of operation and additional principles concerning the status of Commissions with quasi jurisdictional competence. Efforts have been made to ensure that NHRIs are as broadly amended as possible. The Paris Principles set out minimum standards required by national human rights institutions to fulfil their role. The Paris Principles highlight that national human rights institutions must have (a) Clearly defined broad based mandate on universalization of human rights standards. (b) Independence guaranteed by legislation or the Constitution. (c) Insulation from the government (d) Pluralism including membership that broadly reflects the society (e) Adequate powers of investigation (f) Sufficient resources.

The Paris Principles have been endorsed by the UN Commission of Human Rights Resolution 1992/54, March 3, 1992 and the UN General Assembly Resolution 48/134, December 20, 1993. The Paris Principles form the basis for accreditation of National Human Rights Institutions at the international level by the Internal Coordinating Committee. National institutions should be vested with competence to promote and protect human rights. The Principles also envisage that NHRIs will perform a wide variety of functions in promoting and protecting human rights. These include research, public education, promoting ratification of international human rights treaties, ensuring that national legislation, policies and programmes are consistent with international norms and investigating complaints concerning violations of human rights. In some sense therefore national human rights institutions function both domestically and internationally. They are domestic in the sense that the authority to exercise their mandate is limited by their national jurisdictions. They are international to the limited extent that they serve as a national extension of an international order of human rights. The Paris Principles observe that NHRIs should quote, promote and ensure the harmonization of national legislation, regulations and practices with the international instruments of human rights to which the state is a party, and ensure the need for democratic development and viewed as an important part of their effective implementation.

National Commissions can also be the product of peace deals, for example the Northern Ireland Commission was created under the Good Friday Agreement 1998. Some of the peace accords and civil reconstruction missions have also included provisions for the creation or strengthening of NHRIs as an instrument to protect human rights.[4] NHRIs have been considered important for sustained democratic development and viewed as an important part of civil reconstruction and transitional justice. One can take the example of Afghanistan, where the independent NHRC was established in June 2002. It was established through the signing of a decree between the Afghan Interim Administration and the United Nations. The decree vested the Commission with broad scope and competence.

Cardenas has made a useful distinction with regard to the regulative and constitutive functions of NHRIs. Regulative functions of NHRIs ensure conformity with international norms, rules and functions while constitutive functions change the identity of state or societal actors. (Sonia Cardenas, Emerging Global Actors: The United Nations and National Human Rights Institutions, 9 Global Governance 23, 28 (2003). NHRIs should also play a central role in developing good governance policies in states.

Sonia Cárdenas, who has done a useful analysis of NHRCs of India, Philippines and Indonesia has highlighted the dominant role of democracy in the creation of NHRIs. This is striking because the literature on NHRIs focuses on the democratizing effects of NHRIs. Her study shows that states which have created NHRIs are by and large more democratic and have ratified many treaties, report more frequently to treaty bodies and show greater respect for social and economic rights of the vulnerable groups[5].

In view of the critical role played by non-governmental institutions in expanding the work of the national institutions, NHRIs should develop a close relationship with the non-governmental organizations devoted to promoting and protecting human rights.

For investigating complaints concerning violation of human rights the principles envisage that NHRIs should be vested with quasi-judicial powers to compel production of evidence and attendance of witnesses. This will enable them to function effectively. Many NHRIs have lost credibility within their countries by failing to directly take up cases of alleged violation of the right to life and security of the person and the right to physical and mental integrity including the right not be tortured. They have focused exclusively on human rights education or implementation of those rights which involve less criticism of the government.

NHRIs and Courts

Though some NHRIs have quasi-judicial powers they are clearly not judicial bodies and do not purport to make enforceable decisions. They generally make recommendations and proceed less formally than the courts.

However, it is also a fact that courts will not always be sufficient for protection of human rights in many social settings. Various factors impede functioning and impact of courts in dealing with rights-based litigations. Epp Charles in assessing the performance of the Indian Supreme Court with regard to a rights-based litigation, has observed that owing to the limitation of the amount of legal aid available and the way it is administered it is discovered that only 10 per cent of the cases of the Supreme Court belong to this category. Whereas in the United States of America the percentage of rights-based litigation is about 60 per cent[6]. Epp ascribes this to the "weakness of the support structure for legal mobilization, i.e. legal aid, inadequate support for advocacy groups and absence of development of sustained judicial policy making on individual rights.

The quasi-judicial authority has been structured less to provide particular substantive remedies but more to provide a forum that is distinct from the judicial process. This extra judicial jurisdiction has proved to be an effective instrument for addressing issues of systemic violations of human rights.

They also refer matters to other state agencies for further necessary action. The Paris Principles do not offer enough guidance in respect to NHRIs which exercise quasi-judicial powers to investigate individual violations of human rights. However, some useful guidance has been provided in the Commonwealth Secretariat's "Best Practice Manual" (Human Rights Guidelines Best Practice—Commonwealth Secretariat 2001, p. 29). Some of the suggested principles are (a) NHRIs should play a role complementary to that of the courts (b) NHRIs should be accorded standing to bring complaints to courts in their own rights (c) Courts should accord NHRIs official status as a friend of the court. (d) Courts should grant NHRIs the right to join as a party in relevant cases (e) Decisions of NHRIs should be open to judicial review. In many countries courts have been initially somewhat cautious granting leave to NHRIs to intervene as amicus curiae in cases concerning human rights. But in many countries, NHRIs have been able to establish their reputation and credibility and the courts have increasingly relied on NHRIs to assist them in interpreting international human rights treaties or constitutional provisions relating to human rights. For example in India, the Supreme Court has often sought the help of NHRC in enquiring into cases of human rights abuse and sends reports to the court for further follow up action.

The mandate of the Paris Principles has been reinforced on numerous occasions. The International Parliamentary Union (IPU) has repeatedly called upon states to honour the Paris Principles, similarly in 1997; the Council of Europe Committee of Ministers recommended that the government should draw as appropriate, on the experience of existing national human rights commissions and institutions. Thus in less than 10 years the idea of a national institution, distinct from a judicial branch, committed to the protection of human rights has been significantly globalized[7].

World Conference on Human Rights, 1993

The World Conference on Human Rights convened in Vienna in 1993 reaffirmed the important and constructive role played by national institutions for promotion and protection of human rights and in remedying human rights violations and dissemination of human rights information and education. But between the Paris Conference 1991 and the World Conference in Vienna in June 1993, the matter of National Institutions figured for discussions in various regional meetings which were held for Africa, in Tunis, 1992, for Latin America, San Jose, 1993, and for Asia in Bangkok March-April, 1993. Discussions in all these conferences emphasized interest and concern for strengthening of national institutions and encouraged the states to established such institutions on their own. The World Conference called all states to strengthen the national human rights institutions and draw national human rights plans. The Vienna Conference witnessed active participation of national institutions who in addition to their participation in the conference arranged parallel meetings of their own. The

Vienna Declaration and Programme of Action also made references to the diverse activities and positive role played by them for protection and promotion of human rights. The Conference recommended periodic meetings between the representatives of national institutions for sharing experience and examining the ways and means of improving the institutional modalities. The World Conference at Vienna created the post for UN High Commissioner for Human Rights. The decision of the first High Commissioner to make NHRIs a significant area of emphasis prepared the ground for the dramatic expansion of NHRIs activity throughout the 1990s. The World Conference was also significant as it was the first major United Nations Conference in which NHRIs were allowed to speak in their own right. A handbook on the establishment and strengthening of national institutions was drafted by the United Nations to provide guidelines. It is an outcome of thorough research and consultation with a number of national institutions. Thus the national institutions have moved to the centre stage in the strategy to promote and protect human rights and give meaning to the implementation of human rights standards and instruments at different levels. National institutions have become important because they can decentralize, depoliticize and democratize the spread of human rights and create a universal culture of human rights.

Limitations of the Paris Principles

The Paris Principles were originally conceived as minimum standards for the establishment of national commissions. But in reality they have now become the "essential basis" for national institutions. They constitute a maximum programme that is fully met by a few national institutions. This transformation was accelerated by the recognition of the rights of each state to choose the framework suitable to its needs. As a result, there are various national institutions with frameworks and mandates that are strikingly different from each other. It is a fact that many state governments have created national institutions as a low cost way to enhance their international reputation. Such "sham" commissions do not really serve the purpose of protecting and promoting human rights. It is also a fact that NHRIs cannot fulfil their function effectively in states that do not have the "minimum level of democratic governance".

However, the global standards provided by the Paris Principles permit a comparative assessment of the quality of these institutions. A special United Nations Committee, the International Coordinating Committee for the Promotion and Protection of Human Rights (ICC) conducts some accreditation processes to assess whether different national institutions are operating in compliance with the Paris Principles. Institutions deemed to fully comply with Paris Principles receive an "A" classification. Institutions who do not fully comply with Paris Principles receive a "B" or "A", observer status. Non-compliant organizations are awarded a "C" classification. A classification enables an NHRI to become a member of ICC and participate in various activities such as sessions of the Human Rights Council.

Endnotes

1. Economic Resolution 772B of July 25, 1960.
2. Resolution 33/46 of December 14, 1978.
3. Resolution 48/134 of December 28, 1993.
4. Reif C. Linda, 'Building Democratic Institutions: The Role of National Human Rights Institutions in Good Governance and Human Rights Protection', *Harvard Human Rights Journal,* Vol. 13 Spring 2000.
5. See Cardenas, Sonia, Adaptive States: 'The Proliferation of National Human Rights Institutions', Carr Centre for Human Rights Policy Working Paper T-01-04, pp. 17-20.

6. Epp Charles R., *The Rights Revolution: Lawyers, Activists, and Supreme Courts in Comparative Perspective*, The University of Chicago Press, Chicago and London, 1998.
7. See Anna-Elina Pohjolainen, *The Evolution of National Human Rights Institutions: The Role of the United Nations*, The Danish Institute For Human Rights (January 2006).

3
Early Years

NHRC was fortunate in having Justice Ranganath Mishra as its first Chairman. Handsome, light skinned, with sharp aquiline features and with a silvery mane, Mishra looked every inch a judge. He carried himself with great dignity and was unfailingly kind, courteous and compassionate. He spoke in a low tone and weighed every word he uttered. He was clear and crisp in his articulation and could go into the heart of a matter very quickly.

Because of his dynamism, the Commission had a flying start. As happens in any new organization, there were initial teething problems but he was able to handle them with remarkable finesse. Whenever we encountered any roadblock we could go to him and seek his intervention to get matters sorted out. He was also a charismatic leader and had the unique capacity of carrying a heterogeneous team with him. In the Commission, we used to witness clashes of personalities as well as sharp differences of opinion. Sparks used to fly. Mishra, when needed, would apply the healing balm. He was a wonderful coordinator and had natural talent. In my long career in law enforcement, I have come into close contact with many bureaucrats, police officers and judges, but I have seldom seen a more charismatic leader than Justice Mishra. Orders passed by him were invariably clear and crisp and he always took note of the ground realities as well as the practical difficulties of the field officers and issued directions which were clear and very precise. Other Members of the Commission, Ms. Fatima Beevi, Justice S.S. Kang, Justice V.S. Malimath and Virendra Dayal were all persons of eminence and dignity. It was, however, clear that Kang and Fatima Beevi took things somewhat easily and functioned in a relaxed and laidback style. Mishra, on the other hand, was driving the officers of the Commission hard and wanted to make the Commission's presence felt all over the country. He always believed that the Commission's credibility and stature would improve with practicable and well-conceived initiatives for promotion and protection of human rights. He was doubtless a source of inspiration to the officers working in the Commission. Later on, Kang and Fatima Beevi, during the United Front Government at the Centre joined as Governors of Kerala and Tamil Nadu, respectively. Their appointments justifiably triggered controversies. There were legitimate criticisms from different quarters, and particularly, from NGOs, that Members of the Commission while serving in the Commission or after demitting office, should not accept such carrots. This will enable the government in insidious ways to influence the Members of the Commission. These appointments seem to contravene Section 6 (3) of the Protection of Human Rights Act, 1993, which states, "On ceasing to hold office, a Chairman or Member shall be ineligible for further employment under the Government of India or under the Government of any State."

Justice Malimath, before joining the Commission served as the Chief Justice of the Karnataka High Court and Kerala High Court and then as the Chairman of the Central Administrative Tribunal. He had a logical and analytical mind and a great capacity to go into details. However, he never missed the wood for the trees. Once at a meeting, while complimenting him, I said that he could see visions with one eye and details with the other. He was always warm, responsive and sympathetic and many of us in the Commission in times of stress and strain would turn to him for counsel and invariably got from him right and sound advice. After completing his term in the Commission with great distinction, Malimath joined as the Chairman of the Criminal Justice Reforms Commission set up by the Government of India. The report of the Commission, which contained some sound and practical recommendations for reforms of the criminal justice system sparked off angry protests. Many lawyers and human rights activists accused him of pro-police bias and bitterly berated some of the salient recommendations of the Commission. Because of opposition of entrenched interests and inadequate public knowledge, an opportunity to bring about overdue changes in the criminal justice system was passed up. Many lawyers and human rights activists felt that some recommendations of removing restrictions on exercise of police powers would enable the police to act irresponsibly and endanger the rights and liberties of the citizens and help the government of the day to misuse the police. The recommendations based on sound pragmatic reasons, thus, remained unimplemented.

Virendra Dayal served in the United Nations in different capacities over a number of years and enjoyed a well-earned respect for his knowledge and professional competence. A scholarly and straightforward person, he was passionately committed to the cause of human rights. His knowledge of the rules and procedures of the United Nations and association with the leading lights of the human rights movement was an invaluable asset for the Commission. He was also an excellent penman and the annual reports of the NHRC bear the stamp of his facile pen. He also had many excellent ideas about the promotion and propagation of human rights but failed in his action to follow them through—an angel beating his wings in a void.

The Protection of Human Rights Act provided that the central government would make available to the Commission, an officer of the rank of the Secretary to the Government of India, who would be the Secretary General of the Commission. The Secretary General would remain in charge of the administrative apparatus of the Commission. The first Secretary General of the Commission was R.V. Pillai, an IAS officer of the 1962 batch. Pillai was conscientious, committed as well as earnest. He was not very assertive or aggressive but could be firm and persuasive. He had a tough time in setting up the administrative infrastructure of the Commission and persuading some of the Members who at times, could be sensitive as well as abrasive. Section 11 of the PHRA provides for the appointment of an officer of the rank of Director General of Police to head the Investigation Wing of the Commission. I joined as the Director General (Investigation) in June, 1994.

After I joined the Commission, the Chairperson told me that my first and foremost responsibility would be to set up quickly an investigation wing of the Commission from scratch. At that time, my stenographer and I were the only two personnel of the Investigation Wing of the Commission and my job was to pick up and train and reorient investigating officers for the new type of responsibility. The Chairman as well as other Members of the Commission were of the clear view that the fledgling Commission, in order to make its presence felt, must be armed with an efficient and effective Investigation Wing, which should be able to take up investigation of important cases from the very beginning and inspire confidence in the minds of the complainants. Investigation done by the staff of the Commission should not only be non-partisan and above board but also bear the stamp of professional expertise. For this, it was essential to induct in the Commission investigators with a good track record and proven competence. And this was not an easy job.

The Ministry of Home Affairs, which was the nodal Ministry for the NHRC, was of the view that a skeleton Investigation Wing would meet the needs of the Commission. Many officers in the Home Ministry were of the view that the NHRC on its own would not have to take up investigation of several cases. When required, it could, as provided under Section 14 of the Protection of the Human Rights Act, use the services of officers of any investigating agency of the central or state government. This was, however, a most myopic view. I could well foresee that the Commission would soon be inundated with complaints of violation of human rights emanating from all over the country and it must have a well-set and well-trained investigation wing with adequate staff, to cope with such a situation. It would be unworthy of the Commission to depend on the investigating staff of other agencies to investigate into cases reported before it.

A proposal for sanction of staff in the ranks of Superintendents of Police, Deputy Superintendents of Police, Inspectors, Sub-Inspectors and Constables prepared by me and approved by the Commission was sent to the government. The Ministry of Home Affairs raised a host of objections on predictable lines. It felt that there was no need to sanction the posts of Deputy Superintendents of Police and Inspectors. The Commission was pressing me to take up investigation of some cases of egregious violation of human rights and bereft of staff support, I was nowhere in a position to do so. I was feeling helpless. To end the logjam, I met the Chairman and told him that without his intervention, the stalemate would persist and the

Investigation Wing would continue to function without the requisite staff. Mishra's intervention was quick and decisive. He expressed his annoyance to the Cabinet Secretary and the Minister of State for Finance in a no uncertain manner and said that this delay in sanctioning the staff strength was impinging on his work as the Chairman of the Commission. I got to know that he followed the matter up by speaking to the then Prime Minister of India, P.V. Narasimha Rao. The effect was instantaneous. Bureaucratic hurdles collapsed like ninepins and our proposal was accepted with minor alterations and the staff was sanctioned. Without his determined intervention, the staff sanction would have taken an unconscionably long time. Years have rolled by, but since then, no additional staff for the Investigation Wing for the Commission has been sanctioned, though the workload has increased almost exponentially. Indeed, this has seriously impaired the case investigation work of the Commission.

Initially there were protests and misgivings from many quarters regarding the work and role of the Commission. Some of them emanated from old prejudices and some due to lack of information. Some of the NGOs, including Amnesty International, had expressed misgivings about posting of a police officer as a head of the investigation wing of the NHRC. There were expressions of unconcealed fear and anxiety that a police officer would try to whitewash lapses of other police officers charged with serious violation of human rights. Further, investigation done by officers with a police background would not carry conviction and provoke public antipathy. However, this kind of fear, though understandable, was somewhat misplaced. Indeed, police officers working in the CBI or in the state CID conduct whenever necessary investigations against other police personnel for their various acts of malfeasance. Some of the notorious police scandals have been unmasked by police officers working in the CBI. Moreover, investigation by the Commission's officers would be scrutinized by Members of the Commission, some of whom held the highest judicial positions.

Many NGOs also felt that in the investigation wing there should not only be police officers or former police officers but also investigators with different backgrounds like academics, lawyers, etc. who cannot be accused of pro-police sympathies. This view, though unexceptionable, could not be implemented in practice because it was difficult to get lawyers and academics in the pool of investigators. No one was willing to come either on deputation or permanently join the Commission, despite all their professed sympathies for the cause of human rights. Later on however, we were able to ensure during investigation of some specific cases assistance of some NGO groups. They rendered invaluable assistance.

It is true that initially the officers who joined the investigation wing were not seasoned and capable investigators. Serving police officers were reluctant to come to the Commission on deputation because of lack of facilities and creature comforts. Officers, who came on deputation from the Intelligence Bureau, Central Industrial Security Force, Border Security Force, and Railway Protection Force did not have adequate experience of investigating complicated criminal cases. But they were a committed lot. During my innings of slightly more than four years as the Director General of the Commission, I did not receive any complaints of corruption or misconduct against any one of them. The staff of the investigation wing moving in the far-flung areas of the country brought the Commission nearer to the people. The Commission became effective because the team worked well. The Commission also appreciated the commendable work done by the investigation wing. Later on, Mishra in his foreword to my book *Police in a Democratic Society* wrote the following:

"Mr. Sen perceived the requirements of the job in the right way. He soon groomed an excellent team of investigators. He taught them gentle behaviour, adequate grip and firmness in dealings and deft handling of every matter. Within three months visible results appeared. Investigation was the point where the Commission came close to the people, and if the team worked well, the Commission became effective."

Bijbhera Incident

One of the important cases that NHRC immediately after its constitution took up was the case of firing by the security forces in Bijbhera, in Jammu & Kashmir, resulting in the death of about 60 persons. On November 1, 1993, the Commission took suo motu cognizance of the press reports of about 60 people's death in and around Bijbhera as a result of firing by the security forces. It called for reports from the Ministry of Defence, Ministry of Home Affairs and the Government of Jammu & Kashmir. U/s 19 of PHRA, the NHRC cannot directly enquire into complaints of human rights violation by the armed forces, which also include the para-military forces. The Ministry of Defence clarified that the army was not involved in the incident. The Ministry of Home Affairs sent a report on the basis of a magisterial enquiry ordered by the state government and the staff court of enquiry ordered by the BSF authorities. The Commission on perusal of the report felt that it was not at all comprehensive and further study of the evidence of the witnesses was called for. Evidence of witnesses and other materials were made available to the Commission. The Commission carefully studied them. After careful study of the evidence and all the other relevant material the Commission made the following recommendations.

1. The Commission noted that disciplinary proceedings have been initiated against 14 members of the BSF under the Border Security Force Act and further on the basis of the Magisterial enquiry steps may be taken to launch prosecution. The Commission expressed the hope that proceedings should be finalized speedily and guilty officers brought to book early. Payment of compensation on a graded scale was recommended for the next of kin of those killed in firing. It was further recommended that a thorough review should be undertaken by the government of the circumstances and conductions in which the units of the BSF are deployed and expected to operate in situations involving only the civilian population.
2. The Commission was subsequently informed by the government that its recommendations had been accepted. The Jammu & Kashmir government disbursed an ex gratia relief of Rs. 1 lakh each to the next of kin of the 31 civilians killed in firing and the amount of Rs. 25,000 each was paid to 44 injured persons, Rs. 5,000 each to 26 persons and Rs. 1,000 each to 5 persons. This was in the nature of interim relief to the victims and would be adjusted against the final relief on completion of the proceedings.

Review of the BSF Deployment

The Commission was also informed that the central government had issued instructions to DG-BSF that, notwithstanding the complex and difficult security environment, the BSF personnel were required to operate in the state to take necessary steps to ensure that no unit or formation of the BSF resorts to indiscriminate use of force. On receipt of the recommendations of NHRC a further review was undertaken by the MHA along with DG-BSF, advisor to the Governor Jammu & Kashmir. DG-BSF informed the Commission that the following steps have been taken to ensure safety of the civilian population and engender respect for the civilian lives.

(a) The training syllabus of the BSF personnel emphasizes respect for human rights and humanitarian laws, and how to deal with the public, particularly, with the elders, ladies and children.

(b) Whenever cordon and search operations are conducted, the services of magistrates and civil police are requisitioned to help during such operations.

(c) The number of supervisory officers is being increased and special stress is being given to their close interaction with men.

(d) Strict instructions are being given to officers and men to adhere to the principle of minimum use of force. BSF troops are being rotated after every two years so that they do not get overstressed and do not over-react in similar situations.

(e) DG-BSF also informed the Commission that pre-induction training is being given to each unit for four weeks before actual deployment for internal security duties.

(f) Further, to establish a rapport with the public and obtain support of the civilian population, BSF has established a number of dispensaries in the areas of their operation to provide medical aid to the civilian population. BSF is also distributing essential commodities like kerosene, sugar, etc. to the needy population of the affected areas.

Unfortunately, subsequent developments were discouraging. In a letter dated November 12, 1996 A.K. Tandon DG-BSF informed the Commission that the General Security Force Code (GSFC) trial was conducted in respect of 12 BSF personnel involved in the said incident but the confirmation of the trial was being withheld as additional ROE was conducted against Sub-Inspector Mahar Singh u/s 302 of the Ranbir Penal Code as applicable to the State of Jammu & Kashmir.

Later on, the Commission was intimated by the Ministry of Home Affairs that all the BSF personnel involved in indiscriminate firing had been exonerated because the charges against them could not be substantiated. Many of the witnesses did not turn up to depose before the BSF court of enquiry. The Commission wanted to see the proceedings of the trial conducted by SCOI and the record of the administrative proceedings. The Ministry of Home Affairs, however, did not honour this request. In a letter dated May 5, 1998, the Joint Secretary Ministry of Home Affairs informed the Commission of the inability of the Government of India to show the records of GSFC to any authority other than those provided under the Border Security Force Act. In view of the response of the Home Ministry, the Commission referred the matter for an expert opinion to Rajiv Dhawan, a senior Supreme Court advocate and issued an order that the "opinion be brought to the notice of the Ministry of Home Affairs and to send the records called from them to the Commission in confidence for its perusal and necessary action without any further delay."

Unfortunately, there was no response from MHA. The Commission then, in an order dated January 11, 1999 recorded that the Ministry of Home Affairs had not yet forwarded the records asked for and directed issuance of a 'conditional summons' for the personal presence of the Home Secretary before the Commission with the stipulation that in case the records were made available before the stipulated date, the requirement of personal presence could stand dispensed with. A Joint Secretary of Home Affairs responded stating that, "its position was the same. According to the Act, a report based on facts from BSF on the incident, including, action on the delinquent person as per the General Security Force Code (GSFC) was transmitted to the Commission. The Commission then clearly and unambiguously asked the government that all records relevant to the incident should be preserved as the Commission intended to move to the Supreme Court of India.

The Commission then brought the matter before the Supreme Court of India and requested the apex court to issue a writ "to make available to the petitioners, the records of the court martials conducted in respect of the persons involved in the incident" and "to declare that the petitioner must have access to all the public documents that in its opinion are relevant to be perused to arrive at a just and fair determination of a complaint."

The Ministry of Home Affairs took the stand that the "General Security Force Court is deemed to be a court under the provisions of Section 345 CrPC and any trial by the court will be deemed to be a judicial proceeding under Section 193 and 223 of the Indian Penal Code. Once the proceedings have been confirmed by the competent authority and promulgated as per Section 107 of the BSF Act, the proceedings have to be followed in all respects. There is no provision in the Act to show the proceedings to any other party, except those provided in the Act." The Home Ministry, thus, expressed its inability to send the proceedings of the case to the National Human Rights Commission.

The Commission was of the clear view that justice was not done in this case of tragic loss of lives and wherein the Commission had made specific recommendations. The NHRC found it difficult to accept the contention of the Ministry of Home Affairs. It felt that the non-supply of court records would seriously undermine the jurisdiction of the Commission and weaken its scope to operate properly under Section 19 of the Protection of the Human Rights Act. Implicit in Section 19 of the Protection of the Human Rights Act, is the duty of both the government and the Commission, to cooperate with each other to deal with the issue of violation of human rights by the Armed Forces. Such a spirit should animate interpretation of Section 19 of the Act. The Commission felt that in sensitive cases relevant records can be perused in confidence after mutual discussions. The Commission also strongly felt that the stance of the Ministry of Home Affairs was uncooperative and unhelpful. The Commission decided to approach the Supreme Court with a writ petition. It asked the Union Government to preserve all records pertaining to this case.

However, the Commission later on decided to change its stand and withdrew the case from the Supreme Court. The hard and unfortunate fact, however, remains that the Ministry of Home Affairs, the nodal Ministry for the NHRC, did not cooperate with the Commission in this case where several civilians were killed due to indiscriminate firing by BSF personnel and the General Security Force court trial in the BSF exonerated everyone. It was indeed a great travesty of justice.

VIP Security

In September 1993, Jaya Govinda from UP in a petition before NHRC referred to excessive as well as abusive security measures adopted during the visits of VIPs which caused untold inconvenience to the members of the public and amounted to serious violation of human rights. In his complaint, he referred to a visit of the President of India to Jaipur and the excessive security arrangements made by the state government during his visit. He highlighted this particular incident against the backdrop of inconvenience and sufferings of the people due to excessive and obtrusive security arrangements made during the visits of the VVIPs.

Over the petition of Jaya Govinda, the Commission issued notices to all the States and the Union Territories to seek their response. Replies received from many of the state governments were hackneyed and stereotyped and repeated the old stock arguments that it is the prime responsibility of the state government to provide security to the Prime Minister, the President and other VIPs who face risk to their lives by virtue of the offices held by them. Some of the state governments such as Kerala conceded that it is possible in particular situations that the police might have over-reacted and the state government had issued instructions to the police officials performing VIP duties to cause minimum inconvenience to the members of the public. It was interesting to note that the reply received from the MHA related only to the specific incident in Jaipur and did not answer other important and wider issues raised in the complaint. Besides the complaint petition of Jaya Govinda, the NHRC received some more representation and complaints which graphically described how the traffic and the tempo of life stood paralyzed for hours during the movements of the VVIPs. There also prevailed widespread resentment and disgust of the public against the heavy-handed, and at times, rude behaviour of the security personnel engaged in VVIP security duties.

Meeting with the Experts

Before formulating its response and for evaluating the pros and cons of the question, the Commission had a meeting with some of the experts on the subject of VIP security, like K.F. Rustamji, former Director General, Border Security Force and former Chief Security Officer of the Prime Minister, G.C. Dutt, former Chief Security Officer of three successive Prime Ministers, and Arun Bhagat, the then Director, Central Bureau of Intelligence. During discussions, it was pointed out by the experts that police personnel deployed in VIP duties are not properly trained and sensitized and very often behave callously and crudely causing avoidable inconvenience to the members of the public and during visits of the VVIPs, traffic movements in the cities come to a halt. Further, as many VVIPs are not punctual in attending their programmes, traffic arrangements are totally thrown out of gear, creating utmost confusion. Many vehicles are held up at various road corners and intersections causing pollution and health hazards.

Rustamji suggested that whenever possible, VVIPs should undertake helicopter trips from the alighting point to the various places they want to visit. Places where VVIPs stay like Raj Bhavan, Rashtrapati Bhawan, etc., should have their own helipads to facilitate chopper rides and thus reduce road journey hazards. Rustamji also expressed the view that no amount of security arrangements can be a substitute for proper collection of intelligence. However, assassinations of important political leaders in the country reveal the gaps in our intelligence system. He was of the view that political leaders should avoid public meetings as far as possible and should use electronic media to air their views like what is being done by political leaders in the United States of America.

The Commission communicated its views on the subject to the government and recommended that maintenance and enforcement of VIP security had to be done with greater sensitivity and should not militate against the basic human rights of the citizens of the country.

Conditions of Chakma and Hajong Refugees Settled in Arunachal Pradesh

NHRC received representations from the People's Union of Civil Liberties (PUCL) and Amnesty International regarding the plight of Chakma and Hajong refugees living in Arunachal Pradesh. It was stated that these groups comprising Buddhists and Hindus, due to religious persecution fled from Chittagong hill tracts—what was formally East Pakistan, between the years 1964-1971. Initially, welcomed in India and parts of NEFA, which today form Arunachal Pradesh, they were now increasingly being harassed and threatened in this state by the local population. While some of them tried to flee to Assam, it was alleged that the government of Assam threatened to shoot them if they tried to do so. Representatives of the Chakmas, who had come to Delhi met the Chairman of the NHRC and handed over a representation containing their allegations.

The Commission in a communication to the state government on September 29, 1994, stated that it was the obligation of the state government to accord protection to the person and property of the members of the two communities and to ensure that their human rights were not violated. The Commission further called upon the state government to take prompt action to restore normalcy. It also urged the Ministry of Home Affairs, Government of India, to ensure that effective action should be taken by the state government to protect the human rights of the beleaguered groups.

The "Committee for Citizenship" of the Chakmas in Arunachal Pradesh also sent a representation to the Commission asserting that while the Chakmas and Hajong communities settled in other North-Eastern States of India were enjoying the full-fledged rights of Indian citizenship, those settled in Arunachal Pradesh were not being granted such citizenship because of the state government's adamant opposition to the central government's policies in this respect. In consequence, the Committee stated, human rights abuses were being constantly perpetrated against the Chakmas in Arunachal Pradesh. In respect of this complaint, too, the Commission called for reports from the state government and the Home Ministry.

However, in October 1995, the Commission received further complaints regarding violation of the human rights of the Chakmas owing to state-organized violence. Quit notices had been served on the Chakma populace. Recognizing the gravity of the situation, the Commission decided to approach the Supreme Court of India in a writ petition. The Commission's petition sought enforcement of the right to life of the Chakmas and Hajong refugees whether they were citizens or not who were now being threatened by the lawless elements of Arunachal Pradesh. The Supreme Court allowed the petition and in its judgment on January 9, 1996, held that there was existence of clear danger to the lives and personal properties of the Chakmas. The court upheld that the Chakmas had migrated from Bangladesh and had settled in Arunachal Pradesh for two decades. The idea of uprooting them through use of force was contrary to laws and rules. In a country, governed by the rule of law, where every citizen is entitled to equality before the law and equal protection of law and so no person could be deprived of his life and liberty except according to the procedure established by law. The court directed the Arunachal government to ensure that the life and liberty of each and every Chakma residing within the state be protected and any attempt to drive them out of the state or forcibly evict them by organized groups such as the All Arunachal Pradesh Students Union (AAPSU) must be repelled, if necessary, by requisitioning services of para-military forces. The state government was directed to ask the Centre to provide such additional forces as was necessary to respect the lives and liberty of the Chakmas. The apex court further held that the Chakmas shall not be evicted from their homes and shall not be denied domestic life and comfort therein, except in accordance with law.

The State of Arunachal Pradesh moved an application for modification of this judgment and the Commission filed its objections thereto. The Government of Arunachal Pradesh argued that refugees could not be settled in Arunachal Pradesh without consent and consultation with the local people. The Government of India settled these refugees in NEFA, when no popular or elected government was in power to protect and promote the interest of the local population. It said that while conferring citizenship rights on the Chakma population, the central government should also take into consideration the fact about Chakmas indulging in criminal activities, such as procuring arms and ammunitions and encroaching upon the protected areas. A pragmatic decision was required to avoid any future problem, which posed a threat to the security of the state and tended to disrupt the harmony and peace of the native people.

Again, the Commission received a petition dated December 12, 1997 from the President of the Committee for Citizenship Rights of the Chakmas of Arunachal Pradesh (CCRCAP), New Delhi, Mr. Subimal Bikash Chakma. The petition alleged the denial of franchise rights to approximately 25,000 Chakmas and Hajongs in the Lok Sabha elections held earlier in the year. The petition asked the Commission to send directions requesting the Ministry of Home Affairs to issue a notification declaring that those Chakmas and Hajongs, who were born between 1964 and July 1, 1986 are citizens of India by birth, pursuant to the Indian Citizenship Act, 1955 and are, accordingly, eligible for enrolment in the voters' list. It further prayed that the relevant authorities process applications by Chakmas for citizenship in accordance with the terms of the Supreme Court's ruling of January 9, 1996, (Writ Petition (Civil) No. 720 of 1995).

The Commission responded to the petition by issuing notices to the Chief Secretary Arunachal Pradesh and the Union Home Secretary, calling for reports in the matter. The report of the Government of Arunachal Pradesh mentions that the state government is not competent to amend any central acts or rules. Regarding processing of the citizenship application, it reiterated that the state government had never been against granting of citizenship rights to Chakmas and Hajongs and it had been repeatedly asking the central government for the dispersal of refugees following the process of law. The state government was also bound by the Supreme Court's verdict for the removal of Chakmas and Hajongs in accordance of due process of law and without adopting coercive measures. It again reiterated that the law and order situation was peaceful and under control and no complaints had been voiced by the Chakmas or Hajongs regarding any threats to the life and property. The Commission, on a consideration of a report of the central government and Government of Arunachal Pradesh and on the strength of the assurance to comply with the directions of the Supreme Court held that no further action was needed in the matter and closed the case. The

South Asia Human Rights Documentation Centre criticized this decision of the NHRC and held that the Commission's closure of the case on unquestioning acceptance of the state and the central government's report was unacceptable.[1]

Terrorist and Disruptive Activities (Prevention) Act 1987 (TADA)

From the very outset, the Commission started receiving many petitions regarding flagrant misuse of Terrorists and Disruptive Activities (Prevention) Act, 1987. In this connection, it may be mentioned that when violent terrorist activities convulsed Punjab and threatened the unity and integrity of India, the Terrorists Affected Area (Special Court) Act was legislated. But as an alarming increase of terrorist activities made functioning of the special courts difficult, the Parliament passed the Terrorists and Disruptive Activities Act (Commonly known as TADA). It was enacted in 1985, as a temporary provision for two years to enable the government to cope with the rising terrorist violence in the Punjab. The Preamble of the Act stated, "special provisions are made for the prevention of and for coping with terrorist and disruptive activities and the matter connected therewith and incidental thereto".

It was originally enacted for two years and then extended from time to time. The activity which was sought to be punished under TADA could not be classified as a mere law and order problem. The disturbance was to be of such a grave magnitude that could not be tackled by law enforcement agencies through original penal laws. The draconian law had certain features which invited criticisms from the jurists and human rights activists.

First, it had been widely misused by the state government and became counterproductive. Not more than 1 per cent cases under TADA ended in conviction. Second, the Act made the availability of bail extremely difficult. Under the ordinary law of the land, a detainee can be held in police custody for a maximum period of 15 days before being transferred to a judicial custody. Under TADA, it was 60 days. Section 19 of the Act restricted the right of the accused to apply for bail only to the Supreme Court. Moreover, the bail applications have to be filed within 30 instead of 60 days. Third, Section 5 of the TADA made possession of certain unauthorized weapons in specified areas an offence, punishable with imprisonment. It created a conclusive presumption arising out of the mere fact of possession, irrespective of the person's intention for using the same for terrorist and disruptive activities.

Anticipatory Bail

The TADA curtailed the provision of anticipatory bail contained in Section 436 of CrPC. It laid down that the designated courts would not have the power to consider application of anticipatory bail. The constitutional validity of the restriction u/s 27 of the Act was upheld in the case of Sampatlal Jain vs. the State of Assam. The court said that the provisions of TADA denying application of anticipatory bail were not in violation of Article 21 of the Constitution. Because of terror and intimidation by the terrorists, it was becoming difficult to record evidence in the open court following normal procedures. Witnesses needed protection from retribution by the terrorists and the TADA provided for in-camera trial.

The Supreme Court in Kartar Singh's case (Kartar Singh vs. the State of Punjab, 1994) upheld the constitutional validity of TADA but also emphasized the need to ensure strictest scrutiny regarding the applicability of the Act. The Court directed that the screening or reviewing committee by the central government consisting of senior officials should be set up for reviewing the TADA cases. Following the directives of the Supreme Court, different states set up review committees. NHRC also started reviewing detections under the TADA cases with the Home Secretaries and other senior officials of the state governments. As a result, the number of cases drastically came down from 60,000 to only 6,400. Before the glare of the scrutiny of NHRC, many senior state government officials admitted that several innocent people had also been unnecessarily framed under the TADA and in many cases, the grounds of detention did not have even the remotest connection with terrorist activities. The state government that misused it most was Gujarat, even though the state was not plagued by terrorism. The Gujarat government had jailed about 19,000 persons under the TADA. It was used flagrantly against different civil society groups as well as bootleggers and other criminals not involved in terrorist activities. Though the state government of Bihar had not even given official notification of the implementation of TADA, some of the Superintendents of Police on their own implemented the Act in their districts.

The Supreme Court in its judgment in Kartar Singh's case, while upholding the constitutional validity of TADA, confirmed wide-scale public abuse of the Act to circumvent legal provisions. The court held, "it is true that on many occasions, we come across cases, where the prosecution unjustly invoked the provisions of the TADA with the oblique motive of depriving the accused persons from getting bail and on some occasions, when courts are inclined to grant bails in cases registered under ordinary criminal law, investigating officers in order to circumvent the authority of the court invoke the provisions of TADA. This kind of invocation of TADA in cases where the facts do not warrant it, is sheer misuse and abuse of the Act by the police".

In order to ensure that TADA cases are registered only after due consideration and application of mind, the Amendment Act of 1998 made it compulsory that an officer of the rank of Superintendent of Police must agree to the registration of an offence under TADA and the Commissioner of Police or DGP must sanction the prosecution after perusing the connected papers and applying his mind. There was also a high decibel campaign that the Act was being used against the minority communities, particularly the Muslims. In a note prepared on TADA, the Home Ministry conceded that the Act was an issue among the minorities. "Though the available data, the note mentioned, does not justify the allegation that the Act is being used against the minorities, it is true that such an impression exists in some quarters".

Besides closely monitoring the manner in which the Act was being implemented, the Commission followed another strategy. When the date approached for consideration of the extension of the life of the statute, it made a direct request to all members of the Parliament, seeking an end to the law. The Chairperson of the Commission wrote a letter (February 20, 1995) to all members of the Parliament stressing that the Act was a temporary piece of legislation and should not be renewed when its life expired on May 23, 1995. (Annexure of the Annual Report 1994-95).

In the letter the Chairman said that the TADA legislation is indeed draconian in character and has been looked down as "incompatible with our cultural tradition, legal history, and treaty obligation........... the Parliament had entrusted the Commission with the charge of promoting human rights and the Commission is finding it difficult to do so unless this draconian law is removed from the statute book".

The TADA was not renewed after its life expired on May 23, 1995. The Commission's bold stand against TADA, though embarrassing for the government, was hailed by the human rights activists all over the country. It was a vindication of the Commission's independence and credibility. Though TADA was not renewed after the expiry of its life, a knotty problem persisted. There were many undertrials, who remained clapped in jails under the provisions of the TADA. They numbered about 6060 on June 30, 1995. To deal with the disturbing situation, the Commission strongly urged that review committees set up in different states must meet regularly to review the pending cases and release the detainees where the evidence was slender.

The Commission also submitted information at its disposal to the Supreme Court in a case seeking certain relief to the undertrials charged under the TADA. The Commission further remained in touch with competent authorities in the centre and states in respect of TADA undertrials with a view to ensuring that various instructions of the Supreme Court in regard to them were acted upon and their fate was not forgotten because the Act had ceased to exist.

The Commission also forcefully opposed its resurrection in the form of Prevention of Terrorism Ordinance 2001. In its opinion the National Human Rights Commission dwelt extensively on different provisions of the Prevention of Terrorism Bill as proposed by the Law Commission in its 173rd Report. It clearly stated that "Undoubtedly, national security is of paramount importance. Without protecting the safety and security of the nation, individual rights cannot be protected. However, the worth of a nation is the worth of the individual constituting it. Article 21, which guarantees a life with dignity, is non-derogable. Both national integrity as well as individual dignity are core values in the Constitution, and are compatible and not inconsistent. The need is to balance the two. Any law for combating terrorism should be consistent with the Constitution, the relevant international instruments and treaties, and respect the principles of necessity and proportionality. The National Human Rights Commission, therefore, reiterates its earlier view in respect of the Ordinance also".

The Ordinance (4 of 2003) was replaced by the Prevention of Terrorism Act (POTA) 2003. The Commission, however, maintained its firm view that a proper balance between the need and the remedy requires respect for the principles of necessity and proportionality. While it is necessary to combat terrorism, counter-terrorism should not be used as an excuse to suspend all the rules of the international law and domestic civil liberties. While combating terrorism, promotion and protection of human rights has always to be kept in view. (NHRC Annual Report 2003-04, pp. 50-51)

Note

1. *Judgment Reserved: The Case of the National Human Rights Commission of India*. South Asia Human Rights Documentation Centre, pp. 8-9.

4

Amendment of the Protection of Human Rights Act

In May 1998, the NHRC set up a seven-member Advisory Committee headed by Justice A.M. Ahmadi, former Chief Justice of India, to review the Protection of the Human Rights Act and suggest amendments with a view to enhancing the effective functioning of the Commission. The main issues proposed by the Commission for consideration by the Ahmadi Committee were:

1. Whether the philosophy of national institutions; their creative and constrictive role in promoting human rights and the key requisites for their effective functioning, particularly in the context of the administrative system in India, are captured and incorporated in the Act?
2. Whether, in consideration of the fact that most of the complaints received by the Commission concern the Home Ministry, the Commission's administrative link should be with the Ministry or with the Cabinet Secretariat?
3. Whether the proviso to Section 1(2) of the Act is appropriate, as the Commission is of the view that any legislation to provide for an additional mechanism to protect and promote human rights is relatable to

entries /13 or 14 of List 1 to the Seventh Schedule to the Constitution?

4. Whether the definition of "human rights" in Section 2(d) of the Act is adequate and happily worded?
5. Whether, in consideration of the resource constraints of small states, a five-member Commission is necessary?
6. Whether Section 14(1) of the Act is comprehensive enough to enable the procedure of inquiry into complaints by "Human Rights Complaints Authorities" to be set up under the Director-General of Police in the states?
7. Whether it is necessary to provide for a power to commit in contempt of the Commission, in cases where there is inordinate delay on the part of the authorities concerned in responding to notices issued by the Commission?
8. What procedure could be evolved for timely response, by the authorities concerned, to the recommendations of the Commission?
9. Whether Section 16 of the Act should be retained in its present form?
10. In the context of a very large number of cases handled by the Commission, whether specific provisions in the Act are necessary to enable conduct of inquiry by a level below the Commission?
11. Whether it is necessary to clarify and lay down the precise scope and purpose of the provisions of Section 30 of the Act relating to the constitution of Human Rights Courts?
12. In view of the delay that has been observed in laying the annual report of the Commission before each House of Parliament, whether a short time limit could be set for the completion of this procedure?

13. How could an appropriate scheme be built into the statute for an effective inquiry by the Commission into allegations of violations of human rights by personnel of the armed forces and para-military forces?
14. How could the Commission be enabled to take up consideration of cases which are more than one year old, against the background of the provisions of Section 36(2)?

The Commission proposes to pursue these issues, which are vital to its effective functioning, on receipt of the report of the Ahmadi Committee.

The major issues which the Commission requested the Committee to examine are listed in the NHRC's Annual Report 1998-99. (p. 25)—The Committee held 15 sittings to work out the possible amendments necessary to improve the functioning of the NHRC. It requested and received suggestions and recommendations from the Chief Justices of Indian High Courts, Chairpersons of different Human Rights Commissions as well as different NGO groups including some international NGOs. It took pains to consult the rules and procedures of NGOs in other parts of the world.

After an exhaustive deliberative process, the Committee submitted its report and a draft amendment bill to the Commission titled "Protection of Human Rights Bill 1998". The Committee proposed numerous amendments intended to remove the administrative and structural impediments standing in the way of the effective functioning of the NHRC. The NHRC forwarded the Commission's report to the Home Ministry, Government of India, but the MHA evinced lukewarm interest in acting on these recommendations, and thus, betrayed its lack of concern for the Commission's autonomy and accountability.

In its Annual Report of 1993-94, the Commission had clearly stated that autonomy and transparency are the twin pillars on which the work of the Commission must be based. It is to remove the ambiguities and impediments concerning its composition and autonomy, that the Commission is recommending certain amendments to the Protection of the Human Rights Act". The Ahmadi Committee made a number of recommendations and some of the salient ones are the following:

1. The Committee recommended an amendment of Section 11 of PHRA, which prescribes procedures for appointing officers and additional staff of the Commission. In order to ensure autonomy of the Commission, it was considered necessary that appointments should be made with the concurrence of the Commission. Both the Secretary General and the Director General of Police, who heads the investigation wing of the Commission and their staff, should be appointed by the Commission. At present, most of the staff of the Commission come on deputation or on transfer from other government departments. The Commission, thus, loses its prerogative of choosing its own staff. In addition, such a system prevents employment of persons from non-governmental sectors and many of whom may have extensive qualifications and can be experts in human rights matters. The Commission's ability, according to the Ahmadi Committee, to function as a credible instrument of justice to the citizens depends on the ability, commitment, exposure and expertise of the staff of the Commission as well as freedom of the Commission to select the staff of its own choice from both government and non-governmental sectors.

2. The Committee proposed amendment of Section 32 of PHRA which provides that "the central government after due appropriation made by the Parliament by law pay to the Commission by way of grants such sums of money as the central government may think fit for being utilized for the purposes of the Act". The Committee suggested amendment of this provision to confer financial autonomy to the Commission in keeping with its mandate and in line with Paris Principles governing the establishment and strengthening of national institutions for promotion of human rights. The Commission wanted through the amendments of the Act to function as an autonomous body in respect of expending such sums of money as it thinks fit for discharge of its functions.
3. The Committee recommended amendment of Section 2 (1) (a) of the PHRA to exclude paramilitary forces from the definition of armed forces. According to Section 2(1) (a) of the act "armed forces" means the naval, military and air forces and includes any other armed forces of the nation. Thus, para military forces are included in the armed forces of the nation. In international fora, lack of jurisdiction over military, para-military and armed forces is pointed out as a serious infirmity affecting the credibility of the NHRC and commitment to human rights on the part of the Government of India.
4. In this connection, it has to be borne in mind that Section 19 of the PHRA removes the armed forces from the investigative purview of the NHRC. This not only narrows the mandate of NHRC, but also implies that armed forces are somehow exempted from acting in accordance with the principles of fundamental rights adumbrated in Part III of the Indian Constitution.

Indeed, to exclude the armed forces from the purview of the 1993 Act is to separate them from the rest of the state. The existing military procedures such as military trials, court martials, etc. provide no justification for exempting the armed forces from the investigative jurisdiction of NHRC. In fact, military procedures will not be replaced by NHRC investigations. Investigation by NHRC of instances of violation of human rights by members of the armed forces will bring in greater accountability and transparency and enhance public confidence in the armed forces. It is also not arguable that opening the armed forces to the jurisdiction of the NHRC would lower its morale and hamper its operational capabilities. On the other hand, this would ensure greater public cooperation and support. If violators of human rights go unpunished, it would encourage them to commit greater atrocities against citizens with impunity and further tarnish the image of the army as a whole.

5. The Commission wanted amendment of Section 1(f) in order to expand the scope of international covenants to include subsequent covenants instead of freezing it in time to 1966. It recommended that international covenant means the "International Covenant on Civil and Political Rights" and the "International Covenant on Economic, Social and Cultural Rights" adopted by the UN General Assembly on December 16, 1966 and any other covenant or convention which has been or may be adopted by the General Assembly of the United Nations. Now, after the amendment of the Act in 2006, the definition of "International Covenants" has been extended to such other covenants or conventions adopted by the General Assembly of the United Nations that the central government may

by notification specify. Thus, this provision does not fulfil the requirements of Paris Principles. It does not even cover the human rights instruments that India has ratified. There is little reason to expect that the central government is going to specify additional human rights instruments for consideration of the NHRC.

6. NHRC recommended amendment of Section 4 of the PHRA that in the case of appointment of a member of the Commission, the Chairperson shall be a member of the Appointment Committee in view of the Chairperson's responsibility for proper functioning of the Commission. The proposed amendment has not been accepted by the government.
7. Section 12 (c). of the Act empowers the Commission to visit "Jails or any other institution under the control of the state government, where persons are detained or lodged for purposes of treatment, reformation or protection" after giving advance notice to the authorities of those institutions. The Commission recommended that the stipulation of "intimation to the state government" be done away with as it is neither in keeping with the autonomy of the Commission nor capable of ensuring an element of surprise over the visit. Now, after the amendment of the Act in 2006 there is no requirement of prior intimation ahead of such visits.
8. Section 13. The Commission recommended amendment of Section 13 of PHRA. Section 13 (a) deals with summoning and enforcing attendance of witnesses and examining them on oath. The Commission wanted that it should be given the power to obtain duly signed statements in order to obviate the situation of a witness refusing to sign the oral statement with

ulterior motive to deny it at a later point of time. The government has not been willing to accept the recommendation.

9. The Committee wanted amendment of Section 13(1) (f) of the act to transfer any of the complaints filed or pending before it to State Human Rights Commissions for disposal in accordance with the provisions of the act. The proposed amendment has been accepted and finds a place in the Protection of Human Rights (Amendment) Act, 2006.

Section 18 (3) of the PHRA empowers the Commission to recommend "to the concerned government or authority for grant of immediate interim relief to the victims and the members of the family as the Commission may consider necessary". The Commission suggested that it should have the power to recommend to the government grant of immediate relief to the victims or the members of the family during "any stage of enquiry". The amendment of 2006 enables the Commission to recommend payment of "compensation or damages to the complainant or to the victims or the members of his family as the commission may consider it necessary".

Amendment of Section 20 of the PHRA proposed by the Commission was that the central or the state government shall lay before the Parliament or state legislature the annual or special report of the Commission with a memorandum of action taken or proposed to be taken on the recommendations of the Commission. The amendment proposed was if the report was not laid before the Houses of Parliament or the state legislature within a period of three months from the date of receipt of the report, it shall be open to the Commission to publish the report. The recommendation was made in view of the fact that at present due to political apathy or other reasons there has been an unconscionable delay in laying annual reports of the Commission before the Parliament or state legislatures. There has been an abnormal delay in making some of the annual reports of the NHRC public because the reports had not been laid before the Parliament for a long period of time. Amnesty International has suggested that there should be a time limit for the Memorandum of Action to be tabled by the government which will go to ensure that adequate importance is given by the government to the issues of human rights.

Section 36. The Commission also recommended amendment of Section 36 which lays down that the Commission shall not enquire into any matter which is pending before a state commission or any other Commission duly constituted under any law for the time being in force. The proposed amendment by the Commission wanted to give authority to NHRC to take cognizance of an enquiry into the violation of human rights, notwithstanding the cognizance by any other commission, either itself or deal with it in accordance with the Act. In keeping with the pre-eminent status of the National Human Rights Commission it wanted to have an overarching ability to oversee the issue of human rights violations and exercise powers of judicial superintendence in order to prevent any miscarriage of justice in any case of human rights violations This has not been accepted by the government

Protection of Human Rights (Amendment) 2006

The new Act has come into force on November 23, 2006. Some of the amendments brought in force by the new act have been dealt within the forgoing paragraphs. In Section 13 of the Principal Act, a new sub section 6 has been inserted. The new sub section provides for *"where the Commission considers it necessary or expedient so to do, it may, order, transfer of any complaint filed or pending before it to the Commission of the State from which the complaint arises, for disposal in accordance with the provision of the Act"*. The Commonwealth Human Rights Initiative in its submission before the Justice Ahmadi Committee had stated that *"CHRI believes that this would create unnecessary delays in the administration of justice as an individual's complaint is transferred from one commission to the next. Rather than try to free the NHRC from its overload of cases by means of transferring cases back to the states, the Act should be amended to provide for more efficient commissions and greater accessibility at the regional level. Establishing a federal framework of regional offices would also allow the central NHRC to delegate particular research projects to more appropriate regions or expert consultants, thus improving the focus on regional issues and coordinating efforts"*.

Under Section 18 of the principal Act dealing with steps after inquiry, the following provisions have been inserted by the amendment:

1. To make payment of compensation or damages to the complainant or to the victim or the members of his family as the Commission may consider necessary.
2. To initiate proceedings for prosecution or such other suitable action as the Commission may deem fit against the concerned person or persons.

The Commission hopes that with the insertion of the above clauses, it will not only get more teeth in bringing to book the violators of the human rights but will also act as a deterrent against commitment of human rights violations.

Another important amendment pertains to the composition of the Commission. According to the principal Act, the State Commission shall consist of a Chairperson and four Members {Section 21(2)}. With the amendment to this Section, the State Commission would now consist of a Chairperson, who has been a Chief Justice of a High

Court and one Member who is, or has been, a Judge of a High Court or District Judge in the State with a minimum of 7 years experience as District Judge; one Member to be appointed from amongst persons having knowledge of, or practical experience in, matters relating to human rights. Further a new sub-section (6) has been inserted under Section 12 of PHRA, which states that two or more state governments may, with the consent of a Chairperson or Member of a State Commission, appoint such a Chairperson or, as the case may be, such a Member of another State Commission simultaneously if such a Chairperson or Member consents to such an appointment.

The amendments of the Human Rights Act indeed fall short of the recommendations of the Ahmadi Committee. Though some small steps have been taken in the right direction, major recommendations of the NHRC to bring about amendment with a view to making the Commission more dynamic, independent and vesting it with power and authority to appropriately discharge its duties under the act remain unrealized.

The Commission in its Annual Report of 1997-98 very aptly observed that "India must be in the vanguard of the global movement of human rights if it is to be true to its own deepest *traditions and aspirations......it must deal with the problems that it faces openly, fearlessly and with integrity; for no country is* blameless when it comes to its record on matters relating to human rights and all must so function if they wish to serve the cause of human rights with fidelity".

5

State Human Rights Commissions

Section 21 of the Protection of the Human Rights Act 1993 provides for constitution of Human Rights commissions in all the states. At present, 21 States Human Rights Commissions (SHRCs) are in place but the posts of chairpersons are lying vacant in a number of Commissions. The NHRC has always been keen for setting up State Human Rights Commissions as it feels that this is absolutely necessary for promotion and protection of human rights all over the country. It has urged that states which have not yet constituted SHRCs should do so at the earliest in the interest of furthering promotion and protection of human rights. It has also pressed for setting up of Human Rights Commissions at the level of union territories. The Annual Report of the NHRC (1994-95) emphasized that "the Protection of Human Rights Act, 1993, provides for a National Human Rights Commission and State Human Rights Commissions. There is no specific mention in the statute on the setting up of Commissions at the level of union territories as well. This militates against a decentralized grievance redressal mechanism through state commissions. The NHRC has strongly felt that the union territories as well as National Capital of Territory of Delhi should have their own arrangements for discharge of certain responsibilities specified in the Act. Accordingly, the Commission has recommended that the Government of India should take steps for evolving suitable institutional mechanisms for the protection of human rights in Union Territories, including, the National Capital Territory[1].

The Annual Report 1998-99 of the National Human Rights Commission states that a communication was received from the government of Haryana in which it has been stated that *"there was no need to set up a Human Rights Commission in the state. In a similar communication, the government of the National Capital of Delhi expressed the view that a separate human rights commission for Delhi has not been considered necessary as the National Human Rights Commission is already carrying out the function that would be performed by state level commission and it might not be obligatory, in legal terms to set up such a commission"*[2].

NHRC, however, advised the Delhi government to reconsider its decision because Delhi is the third highest among the states in respect of complaints filed before the NHRC. Though Delhi constitutes about 1 per cent of the population of the country, it accounted for 6 per cent of the total complaints received by the Commission during the year.

The Chief Minister of Meghalaya informed the Commission that instances of violation in the state have been few and in view of serious financial constraints faced by small states of the north-eastern region, it is not viable to set up a separate human rights commission for each state alone. Instead, he requested that the possibility may be examined of setting up a joint human rights commission for all the states of north-eastern India, including Assam on the pattern of the working of Guwahati High Court. The Chairperson of NHRC requested the Chief Minister to explore the possibility of using the services of the

Chairperson of the Assam Human Rights Commission to function as the Chairperson of the Meghalaya Human Rights Commission as has been done in the case of the Manipur Human Rights Commission (Annual Report 1998-99, p. 55).

The state government of Uttar Pradesh issued a notification to establish a State Human Rights Commission on April 4, 1996. However, in view of the delay in constituting the commission a PIL was filed in the High Court of Allahabad in September 1998. The NHRC was a party to the PIL. However, during the pendency of the writ petition the government of Uttar Pradesh proceeded to cancel the notification u/s 21 (1) of the PHRA, with a view to rendering the writ petition infructuous. However, the High Court took serious objection to this and in March 2000, directed the state government to constitute the state human rights commission within four months.

The report of the National Human Rights Commission (1998-99) says that in a meeting with the members and the Chairpersons of the State Human Rights Commissions on December 9, 1998 the Chairperson of NHRC called for an exchange of ideas for building of appropriate traditions in respect of the institutions and in respect of matters related to financial disciplines and other issues. At the meeting it was decided that:

1. In respect of custodial death cases, the present instruction of the National Human Rights Commission could be changed to the effect that the state authorities could be instructed also to inform the concerned State Human Rights Commissions of custodial deaths in respect of that particular state.
2. Two Meetings between the NHRC and SHRCs may be held every year for exchange of views and ideas, one in Delhi and the other, preferably by rotation, in a state.

3. The National Human Rights Commission may arrange to share information on research with all the State Commissions.
4. Important decisions and rulings of the National Commission may be circulated by it to all State Commissions.
5. In matters of changes in the Jail Manuals, the States Commissions may have discussions with the respective state governments.

Amendment of the Protection of the Human Rights Act

One of the important amendments to the Protection of the Human Rights Act, (Amendment Act 2006) pertains to the composition of state human rights commissions. As per the principal Act, the state commissions shall consist of a Chairperson and four members (Section 21 (2) With an amendment to the sections, the state commissions would now consist of a chairperson, who has been a Chief Justice in a high court and one member, who has been a judge of a high court or a district judge in a state with a minimum of 7 years experience as a district judge; one member to be appointed from among persons having knowledge of or practical experience in matters relating to human rights. Further, a new sub section (6) has been inserted u/s 12 of PHR Act, which states that two or more state governments may with the consent of the chairperson or member of a state commission appoint a chairperson as the case may be or such member of another state commission if such chairperson or member consents to such appointment.

One of the reasons for delay in setting up the state human rights commissions on the part of the state governments, has been the resource crunch faced by states. Further, a small number of complaints of human rights violations being received by some states has been another reason due to which the latter have not been eager to set up state human rights commissions. With the new amendment, NHRC hoped that the state governments would be in a better position to set up human rights commissions in their respective states or two or more state governments may set up joint state commissions as provided under sub-section (6) of Section 12.

A meeting of NHRC and SHRCs was held on November 16, 2007, in which the Chairman of the NHRC emphasized the need for working out joint strategies in collaboration with SHRCs for addressing the emerging challenges. The Chairman stated that the Commission has made a special provision in its own budget to strengthen the SHRCs. He pointed out that with the amendment of PHRA, 1993, the Commission could now transfer cases to SHRCs. He assured that NHRC would constantly extend a helping hand to SHRCs in complaints handling, and in protection and promotion of human rights. NHRC had helped the Maharashtra State Human Rights Commission to implement the complaint management system in April, 2007.

Experience, however, shows that mere setting up of SHRCs will fail to serve any purpose unless there is an improvement of the SHRCs in terms of personnel and resources, including, financial resources. Only properly equipped SHRCs can reduce the burden of NHRC and help it in the task of protection and promotion of human rights. Some of the major inadequacies of many of the SHRCs are:

1. Complaint handling procedures in most of the SHRCs is somewhat poor. Very often, the complainants are not informed about the progress of their cases.
2. Websites are not fully functional and do not provide relevant information regarding the status of cases and action taken on them.

3. Most of the SHRCs do not bring out publications to disseminate information about their functions and procedures and do not create human rights awareness among the citizens.

PHRA lays down subject matters to be dealt exclusively by the National or State Commissions in accordance with the Seventh Schedule of the Constitution. In practice, however, these divisions are not always strictly adhered to. It has been found that the complainants freely seek redress from national or state commissions irrespective of the subject matter of the complaints. It is also seen that instead of proper coordination and cooperation, they often function on parallel tracks, thereby imperilling the cause of promotion of human rights. Further, appointments of the members of SHRCs are often being done by states on extraneous considerations. Many of the Chairpersons and Members of SHRCs have not been able to win the confidence of the members of the public. For a vast country like India, SHRCs should provide a decentralized complaint redressal mechanism and help the aggrieved parties in distant corners of the country to approach SHRCs instead of NHRC in respect of various complaints regarding human rights violations.

Jurisdictional Controversies

It is also a fact that respective jurisdiction of NHRC and SHRCs has not been properly delineated in the Act. Section 36(1) of the PHRA clearly lays down that the "*NHRC shall not enquire into any matter which is pending before the state commission or any other commission duly constituted by law for the time being in force.*" Experience shows that Section 36 has been used to thwart the purpose of the Act. This has been done by bringing the matter before the SHRC or any other commission in a slightly modified manner to block the jurisdiction of the NHRC. Proposed amendments in Section 36 of the Act for providing a certain power of judicial superintendence to give NHRC the overarching ability to oversee issues of violations of human rights and their remedies have not been accepted by the government. The need for NHRC 's oversight over SHRCS is all the more necessary after amendment in the PHRA allowing transfer of complaints from NHRC to SHRCS since 2007-08. The Commission has been on an average transferring 9 per cent of its complaints to SHRCS every year.. Because of inadequate coordination, NHRC and SHRCs have not been able to establish a mutually beneficial relationship. People's Watch, a civil society organization functioning from Madurai, in a report titled "Time to Raise the Benchmarks" has stated that sittings of many of the SHRCs are often postponed or cancelled without prior notice. Many of the staff of the SHRCs have no education or experience or orientation in matters concerning human rights. Record keeping in many of the SHRCs is poor. Some of the SHRCs do not have an investigation team and rely on the state police for all the enquiries. As most of the enquiries are against the police, total dependence on police personnel for enquiries creates serious problems.

Assessment of the Working of State Human Rights Commissions

Most of the State Human Rights Commissions remain inaccessible to the common people and, particularly, those belonging to the marginalized groups. Further, most of the SHRCs operate from comfort zones of the state capitals and have shown no inclination to go down and function at the district level. Human Rights Law Network (HRLN) a civil society group, made a review of the functioning of the state human rights commissions and came to the conclusion that most of the commission's functions are just like "another government department". (*Rugged Road to Justice: A Social Audit of State Human Rights Commission* by Harsh Doval and Mathew Jacob). Websites of most of the Commissions are not functional and most of them are in English, thereby making it difficult for local people to understand them. The most active website, of all the Commissions, is that of the NHRC.

HRLN had studied the functioning of some of the state human rights commissions and came out with some unflattering conclusions. It mentions that the Kerala State Human Rights Commission (KSHRC) has a well kept information centre and website but it has failed to publish annual reports or any significant report on a regular basis. Assam State Human Rights Commission also does not bring out annual reports. It has a meagre budget that barely enables the Commission to pay the salaries of the staff. It is quite common to see the complainants approaching the Commission, supplying their own materials in order to ensure that the work is done[3]. About the Assam State Human Rights Commission the HRLN study has commented: "*Over the years, the Commission has become known for its failure in delivering justice through its orders and judgments. Though not always, the Commission has favoured the government, in most of the cases. Intelligentsia of Assam has viewed the Commission as post retirement opportunities for judges, who have helped the state in their careers as a judge*". Andhra Pradesh has established its SHRC in August 2004, but it has not able to establish its credibility and is viewed as an ineffective institution by academics and activists. At no time has the Commission investigated cases through its own officers and solely relied on other agencies of the state government to carry out their investigation. "It is viewed as a parking lot for retired judges and career politicians".

During discussions with the author, a former DG of Police, who was also a member of the State Human Rights Commission, listed some of the reasons behind the poor functioning of the State Human Rights bodies. His observations were mainly with reference to the State Human Rights Commission of which he had been a Member but apply, mutatis mutandis to other state commissions. First, the Commissions are too dependent on state governments for manpower and infrastructural resources. Very often, the staff are inadequate and even the sanctioned staff are not posted. Second, unsuitable people have been chosen as Members of the Commission on partisan and political considerations. Such Members failed to command confidence and enjoy credibility. He referred to a case of a District Judge who was retired compulsorily but later on appointed as a Member of the Commission. Third, there is enormous delay in sending replies to notices issued by the Commission and reports called for by the Commission. There should be some provisions in PHRA by which the Commission can take action against government officials or Secretary in-charge of the Department for not responding to the Commission's letters and notices as this amounts to a clear case of contempt.

A meeting of the NHRC, SHRCs and nodal officers of states where SHRCs have not so far constituted was organized on 17th August (year to be given). In the meeting financial, functional administrative autonomy of SHRCs, complaint disposals, human rights training programmes were discussed. NHRC's Annual Report of 2010-11 states that a committee has been constituted by the NHRC to look into the issues of evolving basic structures of minimum manpower and financial requirements of SHRCs in order to enable the latter to efficiently discharge their functions[4].

Adequate funding is the crucial requirement of the State Human Rights Commissions. In its absence they are not able to carry out various tasks entrusted to them by PHRA 1993. NHRC's proposed amendments of Section 36 of the Act for providing a certain power of judicial superintendence over the SHRCs and give NHRC an over-arching ability to oversee the issues of human rights violations has not been accepted by the government. The need for NHRC's oversight over SHRCs has become more urgent after the amendment of the Act to allow transfer of complaints from NHRC to SHRCs since 2007-08.

Notes

1. National Human Rights Commission Annual Report 1994-95, p. 29.
2. Annual Report of NHRC, 1998-99, p. 54.
3. *Rugged Road to Justice,* Vol. 1, p. 131.
4. Annual Report of the NHRC 2010-11, p. 139.

6

Armed Forces

The Indian armed forces are excluded from the jurisdiction of the NHRC. Section 19 of the PHRA prevents the Commission from directly investigating into human rights violations by the personnel of the armed forces. Section 17 of PHRA lays down procedures for initiating enquiries into allegations of violation of human rights by public servants. The provisions of Section 19 of PHRA prescribe a different manner in which the Commission is to proceed in respect of allegations of human rights violation by armed forces. It is restrictive compared to Section 17 of the Act. Section 19 enjoins that while dealing with complaints of human rights violation by members of the armed forces, the Commission shall adopt the following procedures:

1. It may either of its own motion or own receipt of a petition seek a report from the central government and after receipt of a report it may either not proceed with the complaint, or as the case may be, make its recommendations to the government.
2. The central government shall inform the Commission of the action taken on the recommendations within three months or such further time as the Commission may allow.
3. The Commission shall publish its report together with its recommendations made to the central government

and the action taken by the government on such recommendations.

4. The Commission shall provide a copy of the report published under sub-section (3) to the petitioner or his representative.

The armed forces are defined in the PHRA as meaning Naval, Army and Air Forces and include any other armed forces of the nation such as BSF, CRPF and ITBP. The NHRC in its Annual Report (1996-97) observed that an amendment to PHRA is required in respect of the manner in which enquiry into allegations of human rights violations by the armed forces was to proceed. The Commission recommended removal of the privileged status of the armed forces and vested the Commission with the authority to directly enquire into violations of the human rights by the armed forces personnel. It noted that unless the government empowers the NHRC to enquire more effectively into human rights violations by the armed forces "it may erode the credibility of the Government of India with regard to its commitment to respect human rights[1]".

The Commission also expressed the view that the protected status of the armed forces *"diminishes the credibility of the Commission and its goal to promote human rights[2]"*. The central government in the 'action taken' report for the year 1996-97 "noted" the observation made by the Commission since it had not submitted any specific amendment proposal, but subsequent reports of NHRC revealed that even when the Commission issued specific recommendations with a view to removing the privileged status of armed forces and bringing the authority to enquire into human rights complaints under the direct control of the Commission, the government dismissed all such proposals as unnecessary. NHRC also reiterated the request that the armed forces must report directly and promptly to the Commission instances of death, rape or torture occurring while a person was in their custody. The Commission said that failure to report such cases in a prompt and accurate manner would lead to an adverse inference drawn by the Commission that "an effort was being made to suppress the truth[3]".

The government responded by restating the procedures given in the PHRA for enquiry into complaints of human rights violation by the armed forces. The government's position was that "the procedure which has been delineated by the PHRA in respect of the armed forces should be followed". (Action taken report 1996-97, June 1998, Section VIII, pp. 8-9). In sum, the government did not accept NHRC's request for being given greater authority on the oversight of human rights violations by the armed forces. The same exchange was repeated in the subsequent annual reports and action taken reports for the years 1997-98 and 1998-99. In the action taken report for 1998-99 the government said that "a procedure for dealing with armed forces different from that provided in PHRA 1993 is not necessary[4]".

A high level committee was set up by the National Human Rights Commission under the Chairmanship of Justice Ahmedi, former Chief Justice of India, where in its report (October 18, 1999) on structural changes and amendments to the Protection of the Human Rights Act 1993, suggested that the definition of armed forces should be amended to exclude para military forces in Section 2 sub-section 1(a). According to the Committee, armed forces should mean Navy, Army, Air Force and not Central Police forces. In international fora, lack of jurisdiction over military and para-military forces is viewed as a serious infirmity affecting the credibility of the NHRC and commitment of the human rights on the part of the Government of India. The committee further recommended the following amendment of Section 19(2). Upon receipt of the report together with the recommendations of the Commission, the central government if it considers itself unable to comply with the same or any part of it shall communicate its reasons to the Commission within a period of three months or such further extended period as may be given for this purpose by the Commission. The Commission, thereafter, shall consider the same and make such final recommendations as it deems fit. Unfortunately, the suggested amendment was not accepted by the government.

The Commission, however, succeeded after prolonged efforts to make the Ministry of Home Affairs and Ministry of Defence agree that its powers regarding payment of immediate relief to the victims and their families under Section 18 (3) of PHRA would cover the armed forces. In case no. 1060/20/2000-01 and another 1061/20/2000-01, the Commission had been approached by the widows of two residents of Ganganagar district, Rajasthan, who had lost their lives at the hands of a BSF constable under the influence of liquor. The Commission issued show cause notice under Section 3 to the Ministry of Home Affairs, Government of India on the liability of the state to give interim relief under Section 18(3) of the Protection of the Human Rights Act, 1993 to the next of kin of the two innocent persons, who had lost their lives at the hands of the BSF constable. In reply, the Ministry of Home Affairs said that complaints of human rights violation by the members of the armed forces are regulated by Section 19 of the Protection of the Human Rights Act and Section 18(3) of the act is not applicable to the armed force like BSF.

The Commission on consideration on the response of the state analysed various provisions of the Protection of the Human Rights Act 1993 and impressed upon the Ministry of Home Affairs, Government of India, that provisions of Section 19 are specific provisions to deal with complaints of violation of human rights by the members of the armed forces and prescribe specific procedures which are somewhat different from the procedure prescribed under Section 17 for enquiry into general complaints. The Commission emphasized that the power under Section 19 is wide in its amplitude and would include without any doubt the power to recommend interim relief to the victims or the members of the family that the Commission may consider appropriate under the Section of the 18(3) of the Act. The Parliament in its supreme wisdom did not place any restrictions on the jurisdiction of the Commission to make its recommendation after the receipt of the report from the central government under Section 19 of the Act. In the light of the Commission's direction, the Ministry of Home Affairs informed the Commission that it had reconsidered the issue and taken a view that interim compensation can be recommended by the Commission in respect of cases relating to armed forces as well. The Ministry of Home Affairs submitted a compliance report regarding payment of compensation amount.

NHRC's proposal for an amendment of the armed forces as given in the PHRA so as to restrict it to Naval, Military and Air Forces and leaving the para military forces from the provision of the protected status has also not been accepted by the government. Thus, the inability of the NHRC to directly enquire into human rights violation by the armed forces has indeed diminished its credibility and created the perception of the Commission being toothless while dealing with the allegation of human rights violations by the armed forces.

Section 19 of the 1993 Act not only narrows the mandate of the NHRC but also implies that the armed forces are somehow exempted from acting in accordance with fundamental rights principles set out in Part III of the Indian Constitution. During discussions on the Protection of the Human Rights Bill in the parliament, the noted jurist Soli Sorabji aptly said exclusion of the military and security forces from the scrutiny of the Commission is the final act of emasculation. He further said that a provision may be made for co-opting in the Commission a high ranking army officer, when it is dealing with the complaints against the armed forces.

It has been argued that if NHRC were authorized to investigate human rights violations by the armed forces it would weaken the morale of the army, as there will be many unfounded complaints or spurious allegations. However, it is important to understand that NHRC investigations will not replace army procedures. All findings of the NHRC based on its investigations are recommendations only. But NHRC's investigation into alleged human rights violations by the armed forces will subject the armed forces to greater accountability and ensure transparency. It would also not disrupt the chain of command as the investigative staff would work in conjunction with those officers within the forces already charged with internal investigation of a similar nature. There is no reason to fear that opening the armed forces to the jurisdiction of the NHRC would weaken its morale. On the other hand, win for it greater public support and cooperation. If violators are allowed to go unpunished, it only encourages them to commit greater violations with impunity, which will tarnish the image of the army as a whole.

Notes

1. NHRC, Human Rights Newsletter, New Delhi, January 2001.
2. NHRC Annual Report 1996-97, p. 12.
3. NHRC Annual Report 1996-97, p. 327.
4. Action Taken Report for the year 1998-99, December 2000, Section 19, p. 18.

7
Police and Prison Reforms

Police Reforms

Since its inception, the National Human Rights Commission started receiving several complaints against the police from different parts of the country. The complaints range from abuse and misuse of power, custodial violence, illegal detention, implication in false cases, etc. Indeed, more than 60 per cent of the complaints before the Commission related to various forms of atrocities by the police. Some of the complaints were false and frivolous, but there were complaints of serious violation of human rights by the police which could be substantiated during enquiries. The Chairman of NHRC and other Members felt that police misdemeanours and misuse of authority cannot be controlled only if some errant officers are brought to book and some compensation is paid to the victims. Police deviance is deep-seated and cannot be controlled without systemic reforms.

Serious complaints of custodial violence by the police were received from various parts of the country. In this connection, it is good to remember that this evil is not of recent origin. As early as in 1855, the Torture Commission spoke of the prevalence of torture in the police stations of Madras Presidency. The noteworthy aspect of this report, though it remains one of the most significant documentations of torture in colonial or postcolonial India and that it was primarily meant to absolve the British of any role in the performance of torture, despite use of violence to ensure continuance of colonial rule. Torture has been both a product of indigenous traditions reinforced by the British system[1].

The Indian Police Commission (1902-03) had also written of "serious complaints against the police and the unnecessary severity with which they discharge their duties and unnecessary annoyance they inflict upon the public".

The Indian police is still governed by the Police Act of 1861, which was based on the recommendations of the Police Commission of 1860. The Commission of 1860 observed that "the organized police as proposed by us will be politically useful". Thus, a ruler appointed police was set up in India. It was expected that after independence India would radically alter the ruler-supportive character of the police and build up a people-friendly force. However, this did not happen and the system which the British created in 1861 with its twin legacy of servility to the rulers and alienation from the public continues even today. The Police Act of 1861 still rules the roost. The control mechanism of the British Raj had survived and reinvigorated by the new political dispensation. Abuse and misuse of police during the emergency was elaborately covered in the reports of the Shah Commission, which emphasized the need to insulate the police from political pressures and influence. After the emergency, the Janata government under Morarji Desai as the Prime Minister, set up a National Police Commission to comprehensively examine the working of the Indian Police. It produced 8 volumes of reports containing many insightful recommendations. Unfortunately, the well-thought-out recommendations of the National Police Commission

(1979-81) received nothing more than a cosmetic treatment at the hands of the successive governments and its important recommendations were put in cold storage.

The National Human Rights Commission strongly endorsed the salient recommendations of the National Police Commission with a view to insulating the police from extraneous pressures and influence and improving the human rights situation in the country. In its Annual Report 1994-95, the Commission recommended that "serious action be taken on the Second Report of the Police Reforms Commission, which in 1979 made a series of proposals which remain highly pertinent even today, including, those suggesting insulation of the investigative functions of the police from political pressures. Without determined action taken on the report, the Commission feared that the daily directions of the Courts, no less than its own recommendations in respect of police high-handedness, would remain palliatives, the illness itself remaining unchecked". The Commission, therefore, press for action in this regard as a matter of priority[2].

The following core recommendations of the National Police Commission were fully endorsed by NHRC.

1. Insulate the investigation wing of the police from extraneous pressures, ensuring freedom in the operational areas of police investigation.
2. Remove the Damocles sword of premature transfers from the heads of the police and assure them of statutory tenure after proper selection.
3. Formation of State Security Commissions to help the state governments to discharge the superintending responsibility under the framework of law. The State Security Commission will have the State Chief Minister or the Home Minister as a Chairman and persons of known impartiality and integrity as Members. The

functions of the Commission shall include evaluation of the performance of the police in the state every year and present a report to the state legislature. It will also function as a forum of appeal and dispose of the representations of police officers regarding their being subjected to illegal and irregular orders in the performance of their duties.

In its Annual Report 1995-96, the Commission reiterated the need to prevent "interference with and misuse of the police by illegal and improper orders from the political executive or other extraneous sources". The Commission further recommended that "this matter be considered, if necessary, at a meeting of the Chief Ministers of all states and union territories and that in the meantime, the central government endeavours to implement these proposals of the Police Reforms Commission in the union territories as an indication of its own commitment to police reforms[3]".

The Commission further added "in reiterating its recommendations on these matters, the Commission would like to make it clear that it is not unalterably wedded to every detail of the recommendations of the Police Reforms Commission. The essential purpose of the Commission is to ensure that the spirit of those recommendations is fulfilled and that the integrity of the investigative role of the police is restored by insulating it from extraneous pressures".

In the meanwhile, another very important development took place. The then Union Home Minister Indrajit Gupta understood the need for police reforms and in a historic letter (April 3, 1997) to all the Chief Ministers, strongly emphasized the need for systemic and structural reforms in the police. In the letter, Gupta deplored "no serious attempt had been made so far to implement some of the basic recommendations of the National Police Commission to bring about changes in police performance and behavioural patterns. On the contrary, quite often, the recommendations of the NPC for police reforms have been presented, perhaps deliberately, amounting to give unbridled power to the police......The popular perception all over the country appears to be that many of the deficiencies in the functioning of the police have arisen due to overdose of unhealthy and petty political influence at various levels starting from transfer and posting of policemen of different ranks. Political patronage quite often extended to corrupt police personnel".

Unfortunately, no Chief Minister took any serious note of this important letter and nothing was done by anyone in pursuance of police reforms. NHRC in its Annual Report 1997-98, (para-3.27) noted with dismay that the central government in its Action Taken Report for the year 1995-96 responded by stating that NHRC recommendations had been forwarded to the state governments for necessary action as police is a state "subject matter within the jurisdiction of the state[4].

The Commission in addition impleaded itself as a party in the case of Prakash Singh vs Union of India in the Supreme Court. Prakash Singh, a former Director General of Police, filed public interest litigation before the Supreme Court asking the apex court to issue directions to the state and the central governments for implementation of the recommendations of the National Police Commission. The Commission impleaded itself as a party to the case and submitted a comprehensive affidavit. This important decision of the Commission was taken by Justice Rangnath Misra as the Chairperson. The next Chairperson Justice M.N. Venkatachaliyaha fully endorsed his predecessor's stand. In its comprehensive affidavit, the Commission highlighted the need for insulating the police from extraneous pressures as well as other structural reforms so that the police are not misused by the ruling party to subserve its narrow political interests. In the affidavit, the Commission also highlighted the need for police accountability, which must go hand in hand with police autonomy. The Commission recommended the following measures to ensure police accountability and make the police more responsive to the rights of the citizens:

1. Mandatory judicial enquiry into custodial deaths.
2. Observance of guidelines in making arrests as laid down by the Supreme Court in the case of Jogindra Kumar vs the State of Uttar Pradesh, (1994, Supreme Court/423). These specific guidelines must find a place in police manuals and other police regulations.
3. Institution of lay visitors to visit jails and police lockouts.
4. Constitution of District Complaints Authority to examine complaints from the public regarding police excesses, false implication in criminal cases, custodial violence, etc. and make appropriate recommendations to the government or NHRC or State Human Rights Commissions.

The Commission promised to extend all such assistance that the apex court may need in the implementation of these measures.

The Supreme Court after a gap of 10 years in 2006 in Prakash Singh's case, issued clear directives to the centre to implement the recommendations of the National Police Commission till a model Police Act was enacted by the government. The 7-point directives of the Supreme Court include:

(a) A fixed tenure for at least two years for Director General of Police (DGP) unless promoted or removed on disciplinary grounds. The Chief Minister will no longer be able to remove or transfer any inconvenient DGP and pick up a pliant officer of his choice.

(b) Separation of the law and order wing and investigation wing of the police.

(c) Setting up of a Police Establishment Board to decide on transfer, posting and service-related matters of the officers up to the rank of Deputy Superintendent of Police.

(d) Setting up of a State Security Commission in every state to ensure that the state government does not exercise unwarranted influence and pressures on the police.

(e) Establishing a National Security Commission for selection and placements of Chiefs of Central Police Organizations.

The Court further ordered that Public Complaint Authority (PCA) will be set up in every district headed by a retired District Judge to enquire into allegations of serious misconduct by the police.

The judgment of the Supreme Court has been historic,, but unfortunately many state governments are dragging their feet and trying to scuttle the proposed reforms in various ways. Most of the states have averred that though they support the spirit of reforms they object to many of the directives of the court. States like Gujarat, Nagaland, Andhra Pradesh and Karnataka have questioned the raison d'etre of state security commissions. Though many states have enacted new police acts, the new acts that have been passed seek to dilute the core systemic reforms prescribed by the Supreme Court. Some of the states have set up State Security Commissions but packed them with yes men and excluded the leader of the opposition to deny the body a bi-partisan character. The Supreme Court however, cracked the whip and set up a three-member monitoring committee with Justice K.T. Thomas, a former Supreme Court judge, as its Chairperson.

The Committee examined all the available documents, including the affidavits filed by the central and state governments before the Supreme Court. It also decided to take stock of the new Police Acts legislated by some of the states, in order to review whether or not they conformed to the Supreme Court guidelines. In terms of compliance no state complied with the directives properly. The Acts contained provisions that violated the Directives of the Apex Court.

The Committee was dissatisfied with the compliance reports of the states and felt the need to look into the ground realities. It decided to visit four states of Maharashtra—West Zone, Uttar Pradesh—North Zone, Karnataka—South Zone and West Bengal—East Zone. On visiting the states, the committee came to the conclusion that there was poor compliance bordering on virtual non-compliance by the states of the directives issued by the Supreme Court. The Committee's clear conclusion was that insofar as the implementation of the six specific Directives of the Supreme Court is concerned, the Committee had no hesitation in concluding that practically no state has fully complied with those directives so far, in letter or spirit, despite the lapse of almost four years since the date of the original judgment. In the states, where new police legislations have not been enacted, the directions are purported to have been complied with by issuing executive orders but the contents of such executive orders clearly reflect dilution, in varying degrees, of the spirit, if not the letter, of the Court's directives.

The Supreme Court has taken up the matter seriously. A bench headed by the Chief Justice adopted a no- nonsense approach and chided the West Bengal government for putting the health minister as the head of the State Security Commission. The Court also severely castigated the government of UP for not segregating law and order and investigation wings of the police. The Court had said that it will not allow its order "to remain in limbo". The path of police reform is going to be bumpy in view of the stubborn reluctance of the political masters to implement reforms which will make the police neutral and apolitical.

An appraisal of NHRC's role for implementation of police reforms shows that the cause of police reforms received a big boost due to NHRC's support. The major recommendations of the National Police Commission, which were lying frozen and dormant for nearly two decades, were again resurrected and revivified. Even many civil society groups which were earlier invariably critical of the police came forward to espouse the cause of police reforms. However, it is a matter of regret that NHRC has not followed up its initial enthusiasm for the cause of police reforms and not acted on the conviction that police reforms are sine quo non for protection and promotion of human rights in the country. NHRC should press state governments and the central government to implement the directives of the apex court and also forcefully urge before the court that its directives must be implemented and not diluted and scuttled.

Prison Reforms

Prisons constitute a critical area of human rights concern. A person in custody in any civilized society cannot be reduced to the status of a non-person because he is in prison. Hence, the prison system must offer conditions that are compatible with human dignity and conducive to social mainstreaming. Article 10 of the International Covenant on Civil and Political Rights (ICCPR) mandates that "All persons deprived of liberty shall be treated with humanity and with respect for the inherent dignity of the person". United Nations Standard Minimum Rules for Protection of Prisoners known as "Standard Minimum Rules" adopted by the UN Social and Economic Council in 1957, provided guidelines for treatment of prisoners and reaffirmed the tenet that prisoners do retain their fundamental rights even while in custody. The goal of imprisonment, to quote the memorable words of Justice Krishna Iyer, in the case of Prem Shankar Shukla vs Delhi Administration, is not only punitive but restorative, "to make an offender a non-offender". Unfortunately, human rights of persons languishing in prisons are often disregarded and violated. There are contradictions and dysfuntionalities at the heart of the prison system. It is aptly said that prison is a place where the ills of society are distorted and exacerbated.

Number of Prisoners

In India, most of the prisons are overcrowded and suffer from appalling mismanagement and lack of adequate facilities. According to Prison Statistics India, the total number of jail inmates on December 31, 2013, was 3,85,135—male 3,68,184 (95.6%) female 16,951 (4.4%). The number of convicted inmates was 1,27,789 (33.2%) of total inmates, under-trials 2,54,857 (66.2%) of total inmates. Thus it can be seen that the under-trials constitute a disproportionate majority of the prison population.

Section 12(c) of the Protection of the Human Rights Act, 1993, authorizes the National Human Rights Commission to visit "under intimation to the state government any jail or any other institution under the control of the state government, where persons are detained or lodged for purposes of treatment, reformation or protection to study the living conditions of inmates and make recommendations thereon". Now, after the Amendment of the Act in 2006, there is no requirement of prior intimation ahead of such visits. In its Annual Report (1993-94), NHRC had on the basis of complaints received expressed deep concern over overcrowding, lack of sanitation, poor medical facilities and inadequate diet in prisons in the country. It expressed its dismay at the reports of delay at the disposal of cases and mismanagement of the prisons in the country.

In India, the prison administration is governed by the Prison Act of 1894. The Act is old and many of its provisions are outdated. Section 27 of the Act provides that un-convicted prisoners ought to be kept apart from convicted prisoners. Many jail manuals also provide for segregation of undertrials from the convicted prisoners. However, there are no separate buildings for keeping the undertrial prisoners. So, very often they are lodged together with the convicted inmates. Lodging of undertrial prisoners with convicted criminals results in "contamination of crime". It is a fact that inexperienced young undertrials coming in touch with hardened criminals get coarsened and many criminal gangs recruit their members from these inexperienced undertrial prisoners. NHRC has strongly felt that for improving prison conditions, determined efforts are necessary to reduce the numbers of undertrials in jails. In a letter addressed to Chief Justices of all High Courts on undertrial prisoners, the NHRC referred to the Supreme Court's decision in the case of Common Cause vs Union of India, (6) SCC775, in which the apex court prescribed different kinds of cases pending trial where the accused persons can be released on bail. Unfortunately, the judgment of the case is not self-executing and even after the judgment many prisoners continue to languish in jails because there is nobody to present their cases before the courts. Further, a number of prisoners, though granted bail, remain imprisoned because there is no one to provide sureties for them. It requested the Chief Justices to issue directions to the Magistrates and the Sessions judges within their jurisdiction to follow up and ensure enjoyment of liberty and freedom of movement for poor undertrial prisoners. In another letter dated July 1, 2003, to the Chief Justices of High Courts, the then Chairman of NHRC Dr. Justice A.S. Anand reiterated the following measures that may be found useful in reducing the number and condition of undertrials in state prisons.

Regular holding of special courts in jails and its monitoring by the Chief Justice/senior Judge of the High Court.

Monthly review of the cases of undertrials in the light of the Supreme Court's judgment in Common Cause vs Union of India (1996(4) SCC 33 and 1996 (6) SCC 775). In this judgment, the Supreme Court has issued clear directions for (a) release on bail and (b) discharge of certain categories of undertrials specified in the judgment.

Release of undertrials on Personal Bonds: A number of undertrials are found to be languishing in jails even after being granted bail simply because they are unable to raise sureties. Cases of such undertrials can be reviewed after 6-8 weeks to consider their suitability of release on personal bonds, especially, in cases when they are first offenders and punishment is also less than 2/3 years.

Visit of District and Sessions Judge to Jail: The Jail Manuals of all the states contain provisions for periodical visits of the District and Sessions Judge as an ex-officio visitor to jails falling within their jurisdiction. Besides ensuring an overall improvement in management and administration of the prison, such visits can help in identifying the cases of long-staying undertrials, which need urgent and special attention. The Commission has observed a marked improvement in the situation in the states where this obligation is being discharged seriously and sincerely by the subordinate judiciary. It would be useful to issue directions for such visits by all the ex-officio visitors to jails falling in their jurisdictions.

The Supreme Court now in a landmark order in Bhim Singh vs Union of India directed the release of undertrial prisoners, who had completed at least half of their maximum prison terms in accordance with Section 436A of the Criminal Procedure Code. The Court highlighted the pitiable condition of the undertrial prisoners. The order of the apex court coincided with the present Narendra Modi government's mandate to decongest prisons by releasing undertrials. At present more than 66% of India's prisoners are undertrials, which is over twice the global average of 32%.

The Annual Report of 2010-11 of NHRC mentions that overcrowding which has been an important factor for determining the living conditions of the prisoners inside the jail had shown a significant decline of 15.5% from June, 2005 (42.9%) to June, 2009 (27.4%). A slight downward trend was also noticed in the percentage of undertrials as it declined from 68.3% in June 2008 to 67.9% in June, 2009.

The National Human Rights Commission made an in-depth analysis of the death of prisoners in jails and came to the conclusion that lives of many of the prisoners would have been saved if proper medical examinations had been carried out at the time of admission followed by periodical medical checks. One of the early directions made by the Commission was that cases of death in police and jail custody are to be reported to it within 24 hours. During the year 2012-13, 1471 cases of death in jail custody were reported to the Commission. One of the major causes of death in jail is tuberculosis because of over-crowding and unhygienic conditions in prisons; many prisoners contract this illness and perish. The National Human Rights

Commission with the help of experts devised a proforma for health screening of the prisoners and directed the Chief Secretaries of all states to ensure that medical examination of all prisoners should be carried out in accordance with this procedure. (Letter of the Human Rights Commission dated February 11, 1999).

The Commission further required that the monthly report of progress should be communicated to the Commission. The Special Rapporteur and Chief Coordinator of the custodial justice programme of the Commission was required to monitor these efforts of the state governments and guide the prison administrators in this matter. The format includes indication by examining a medical officer as to the medical and diet regime that should receive particular attention. Though the prison rules require examination of the prison inmates on or immediately after the admission, conduct of such medical examination is more an exception than the norm.

A frequent complaint which the NHRC gets from the prisoners is regarding the quantity and quality of food served to them. In the restricted environment of the prison, where the prisoners do not get the food of their own choice and liking, the quality of food served to them becomes an important issue. The NHRC officers in the course of their visits to different prisons have found that prison kitchens are dirty and the manner of preparation of food for the prisoners is unhygienic. Many prisoners suffering from diseases and not knowing cooking at all are compelled to cook food. In many prisons, food of inferior quality is given to the prisoners, who fall foul of the prison staff. NHRC has recommended that the ways and means of privatizing catering services in the prison should be examined and the work of preparing food for the prisoners should be given to responsible NGO groups.

In a case reported from Thane Central Jail, Maharashtra, (complaint petition of Jagannath Paoji Ingule), the National Human Rights Commission pointed out that "timely and proper medical diagnosis and treatment is an inherent right of the prisoner. His freedom to seek and have access to medical aid outside is curtailed by law. Hence, the prison authorities are, therefore, under duty to provide reasonable degree of care and facility". The Commission, in this case, awarded an interim relief of Rs. one lakh to the dependents of the deceased prisoner and also directed the Maharashtra Government to make a comprehensive appraisal of the control and spread of tuberculosis and other infectious diseases in the prisons and to install, wherever lacking, adequate diagnostic facilities.

The National Human Rights Commission also brought out draft guidelines for improving prison conditions. In drafting the guidelines, the Commission consulted a number of NGOs involved in practical prison work and also people with long practical experience in prison administration. These guidelines have been circulated to all the Inspectors General of Prisons with a view to bringing about improvement in prison conditions.

Checklists

For practical guidance to the officers inspecting jails the Commission prepared a checklist in consultation with the experts regarding the issues to be kept in mind during inspection. Before finalizing the checklist the Commission sought and got the comments of IGs of Prisons and other experts. During visits to prisons in various states, the Commission Members as well as its officers observed that Session Judges were not visiting jails in a regular manner as required by the prison manual. The Chairperson of NHRC, in a letter to the Chief Justices of all High Courts (letter of

Justice J.S. Verma to Chief Justices of all High Courts dated January 1, 2000) requested them to give instructions to all the District Judges to monitor the living conditions of the prisoners and ensure that humane conditions prevail within the prison walls. He pointed out that judges are not regular in visiting prisons and the District Committees headed by Sessions Judge/District Magistrate/Senior Superintendent of Police is not meeting at regular intervals to review the conditions of the prisoners.

The difficulties of the prisoners in getting parole came to the notice of the Commission in several cases. In one particular case (NHRC case no. 8572/95-96/NHRC) Harbajan Singh, a convict undergoing life imprisonment, in Central Jail in Bikaner levelled corruption charges against the Superintendent of the Central Jail, Bikaner. He alleged that when he asked for the grant of parole to make arrangements for the medical treatment for his wife, the Superintendent of Jail had given a wrong report that the complainant was planning to leave the country. The jail administration in its report to the Commission, admitted that there had been a mix up of papers with the same identical name and the Superintendent of Jail sought to explain it as a clerical error and said that when the mistake was detected grant of parole was recommended to the District Magistrate. The Investigation by the Commission revealed that the Jail Superintendent had asked the complainant's son to pay Rs. 20,000 and made clear that otherwise the complainant's father would face a tough time in jail. After a few months, the complainant's mother expired. The complainant's father managed to get parole by making a payment of Rs. 3,000. The Commission directed the state government to take appropriate action against the jail officials and pay Rs. 20,000 to the complainant because of deprivation, humiliation and harassment suffered by him.

The NHRC gets petitions from life convicts even over 70 years of age, who have been languishing in prisons for more than 30 years. Section 433-A of the Criminal Procedure Code prescribes that "if a person is convicted of an offence for which death is one of the punishments provided by law or where the sentence of death imposed on a person has been commuted under Section 433 of the Criminal Procedure Code into one of imprisonment of life, such a person shall not be released unless he has served at least 14 years of imprisonment". This Section of the Criminal Procedure Code, in the opinion of Justice A.M. Mullah Committee on Jail Reforms had the effect of sacrificing the "values of rehabilitation and reformation on the lifers altogether". In selected cases, the power of the Governor to grant pardon can be effected under Section 161 of the Constitution so that the prisoners can be released even before completing 14 years of imprisonment. However, it has been noticed that even exercise of this power by the Governor for premature release of the prisoners has not been based upon objective criteria.

The Commission also felt that the knowledge of the prison staff regarding prison rules, procedures and the directions of the court is inadequate. Their communication skills and interpersonal management are very poor. The Commission took the initiative in organizing training courses for the prison staff in collaboration with the National Institute of Criminology and Forensic Science (NICFS). The efforts of the Commission evoked a positive response and now regular courses for the prison officials are organized by the NICFS.

It also came to the notice of the Commission that though the powers of premature release of prisoners undergoing sentence of life imprisonment is to be exercised by the state governments under provisions of 432 of the

Criminal Procedure Code, the procedure and practice followed by different state governments are not uniform. The system differs from state to state so far as eligibility criteria of the persons eligible for consideration of release, composition of Sentence Review Boards and the guidelines governing the question of premature release. In many states, Sentence Review Boards have not been meeting regularly. The Commission formed a committee comprising its senior officers and evolved a set of recommendations to bring about uniformity of procedures in all states to be followed. The Commission also issued detailed guidelines regarding the composition of State Sentence Review Boards, periodicity of its meetings and the categories of prisoners, who should not be considered for premature release like prisoners convicted of the offence such as rape, murder, terrorist crimes, etc. and the guidelines are to be followed by Sentence Review Boards.

Women Prisoners

The Commission had given special attention to the condition of women prisoners. Female prisoners constitute a very small portion of the total prison population of the country. This relatively low proportion of women in the prison population has been attributed to various factors like women's innate nature, their domestic status, putative weaknesses and ambiguity regarding their public responsibilities. Unfortunately, this minority status of women in prison tends to reinforce their lost status. The Commission felt that some of the key recommendations of the National Expert Committee on women prisoners which met under the Chairmanship of Justice V.K. Krishna Iyer (1986-87) should be followed up with greater vigour and earnestness.

The NHRC Members as well as officers visiting jails have noted with dismay that there was no pre-release planning and policy for the rehabilitation of women prisoners after their release. This is necessary because women are stigmatized for being in prison and considered as pariahs by the society. A number of women prisoners suffer from mental depression and other forms of psychosomatic illness. There is no arrangement for psychiatric treatment and counselling for them. Prison administration has also to be more responsive to the problems of children of the women prisoners.

The Commission has always placed utmost stress on the human rights sensitisation of the prison staff, particularly the female staff, as well as judicial officers and members of the civil, society groups visiting prisons and interacting with the women prisoners. Their intense sense of loneliness and longing to meet members their families has to be understood and appreciated. Many of the women prisoners need psychiatric counselling o as they suffer from mental trauma and depression. This problem has to be seriously addressed by the prison authorities.

Prison Bill

In the 1994-95 Annual Report the Commission had recommended creation of a new all India Jail Manual as a model for the country. The Commission was clearly of the view that the outdated Prison Act of 1894 must be revised. The Commission circulated a draft prison bill to the states to elicit their views. Unfortunately, there has not been any further progress in the matter and the Indian Prison Act stands as originally passed in 1894. While enactment of a new Prison Act is still pending, the Bureau of Police Research and Development (BPR&D) has revised the Jail Manual largely in accordance with the guidelines given by the Commission in the Draft Prison Bill and a number of states have adopted the same as replacement of the old archaic manual. This has brought about noteworthy improvement in the condition of the jails in the states and also improved the human rights condition of the prisoners.

The Annual Report of 1996-97 the Commission mentioned the fact that the Mumbai High Court in writ petition no. 3899/96 (Muktaram Sitaram Shinde vs. State of Maharashtra) has asked the state government to appoint nominees of the National Human Rights Commission as ex-officio or non-official visitors to jails in that state. Responding to the directions of the court, the Commission nominated persons for the prisons of Maharashtra and the state government subsequently notified them as visitors. The visitors play an important role in keeping watch on behalf of the Commission over prison conditions in Maharashtra.

In a national seminar on Prison Reforms organized on April 15, 2011, the Commission inter alia stressed that:

1. Guidelines of the Supreme Court for the children of women prisoners mentioned in the case of R.P. Upadhayaya vs State of AP and others should be followed strictly.
2. Process of modernization of prisons as devised by BPR&D should be given the highest priority.
3. Self sustainability of prisoners should be encouraged by strengthening the prison industries. The model of Tihar Jail in this regard should be followed.
4. Presence of prisoners in courts should be done through video conferencing.
5. Privatization of some of the duties like catering and escorting of prisoners may be considered to reduce the burden on prison administration. This is being followed in advanced countries.

Notes

1. Torture in Custody: Method in Sadistic Madness by Sumanta Banerjee, *Economic and Political Weekly*, Vol. 36, 2001, pp. 723-724
2. Annual Report of NHRC, para 4(13), p. 12.
3. Annual Report 1995-96, para-3(26), p. 16.
4. Action Taken Report, for the year 1995-96, Section XIII, p. 24.

8

Bonded Labour

It is an unfortunate fact that, despite enactment of the Bonded Labour System (Abolition) Act 1976, the reprehensible bonded labour system in some form or other prevails in the country. "We have to go a long way", said the Supreme Court in Bandhu Mukti Morcha vs Union of India (1984) "to wipe out this outrage against humanity" (1984). In this case the court further said that the "state government cannot be permitted to repudiate its obligation to identify, release and rehabilitate bonded labour on the plea that though the concerned labourers may be providing forced labour, the state government does not owe any obligation to them till they show in an appropriate legal proceeding conducted according to the rules of the adversarial system of justice that they are bonded labourers".

Bonded labour characterized by a long-term relationship between the employer and the employee is usually solidified through a loan embedded intricately in India's socio-economic culture. Bonded labour is a specific form of forced labour, in which compulsion into servitude is derived from debt. It is characterized by a creditor-debtor relationship that a worker often passes to his family members. It is often of indefinite duration and contains illegal contractual stipulations. Bonded labour contracts are not purely economic, they are reinforced by custom and coercion in many sectors. Bonded labour stems from a variety of causes like caste-based discrimination, vast poverty and inequality, unjust social relations and lack of political will to alter the status quo.

The factors which trigger the bonded labour system are crisis or death in the family due to prolonged illness, accidents, natural calamities, sudden loss of employment, etc. Unfortunately, in varying degrees, the state governments ignore or refuse to acknowledge the existence of bonded labour in their states, as they fear that such an acknowledgment will tarnish the image of state administration. Authorities instead of responding promptly to the complaints of bonded labour, try to help the bonded labour keepers to arrange the dispersal bonded labourers after hurriedly settling their accounts.

Though the bonded labour system is deeply embedded in feudal and semi-feudal social structures, it is also prevalent in advance agriculture and non-agricultural sectors. In non-agricultural sectors it is prevalent in brick kilns, stone quarries, bidi manufacturing and carpet-weaving, construction projects, fire-works industry, etc.

International Instruments

Indeed, the system of bonded labour is an outrageous violation of human rights. It is denounced in international instruments dealing with human rights. Article 4 of the Universal Declaration of Human Rights enjoins that "none shall be held for slavery or servitude". Article 8 of the International Civil and Political Rights prohibits use of forced labour. In this connection, it may be mentioned that as early as in 1930, long before the Universal Declaration of Human Rights came into being, the Forced Labour Convention no. 29 was adopted by the International Labour Organization (ILO). ILO Convention defines forced labour as "all work or service expected from any person under the menace of penalty in which the said person has not offered himself voluntarily". Article 2 of the Convention however, lists some forms of forced or compulsory labour which are not banned or regulated by the convention like compulsory military services, services from a person as a consequence of conviction in a court of law. The Supreme Court in the case of People's Union for Democratic Rights vs Union of India and others 1982 (Sec 235) otherwise known as the Asiad Workers case held "exaction of labour and services against payment of less than minimum wages amounts to forced labour and violates Article 23 of the Constitution which lays down that *"Trafficking in human beings and other forms of forced labour are prohibited and any contravention of this prohibition shall be an offence punishable in accordance with the law."*

Provisions of the Bonded Labour System (Abolition) Act, 1976

The Act seeks to abolish the bonded labour system under which a debtor would render service to the creditor in consideration of an advance obtained from him. The main features of the Bonded Labour System (Abolition) Act are as under:

- On commencement of the Act, the bonded labour system shall stand abolished and every bonded labourer shall stand freed and discharged from any obligation to render bonded labour.
- Any custom, agreement or other instrument by virtue of which a person is required to render any service as a bonded labourer shall be void.
- Liability to repay bonded debt shall be deemed to have been extinguished.

- Property of the bonded laborer is required to be freed from mortgage, etc.
- Freed bonded laborers shall not be evicted from homestead land or other residential premises which she/he was occupying as part of the consideration for the bonded labour.
- District Magistrates have been entrusted with certain duties and responsibility for implementing the various provisions of the Act.
- Vigilance Committees are required to be constituted at District and Sub-Divisional levels.
- Offences for contravention of provisions of the Act are punishable with imprisonment for a term which may extend to three years and also with a fine which may extend to two thousand rupees.
- Powers of Judicial Magistrates are required to be conferred on Executive Magistrates for trial of offences under the Act. Offences under the Act may be tried summarily.
- Every offence under the Act shall be cognizable and bailable.

Critical Assessment

Unfortunately, the implementation of the Act has been tardy and poor. There are various factors responsible for poor implementation of the Act. First, there is an endemic apathy among government officials charged with enforcing Indian labour laws. This is apparent at all levels—national, state and district. There are, of course, some committed officials, but they are few in number. The bureaucracy, on the whole, is in favour of the status quo. Second, the failure of the government to implement the Act is most evident in the universal failure of the districts to form vigilance committees, which constitute the core of the enforcement strategy devised under the Act. These committees, if they function properly, can contribute dramatically to the elimination of bonded labour. Unfortunately, this is not happening. It has been found that in many cases, officers entrusted with enforcement strategy, devised under the Act are more sympathetic to the employers than to the child or to the bonded laborers. This phenomenon has been repeatedly noted in the context of the enforcement of the Act. There is delay in processing of complaints and many cases remain pending for years. Again, wherever vigilance committees are formed they have been mostly composed of people themselves either directly or through their families employing bonded labour. Further, the violators of laws often dare to cause overt obstruction of the legal process, ranging from intimidation of the complaining workers, bribery of government officials and physical threats and violence against bonded labourers and their advocates. The danger is greatest in the rural areas, where bondage is often a norm and the powerful and ruthless owners dominate the scene.

Lack of Accountability

Under the Bonded Labour Act, District Magistrates are supposed to periodically report to the state government regarding the number of cases of bonded labourers identified, released and rehabilitated. Most of the District Magistrates do not send reports or send such reports sporadically. Further, no such mechanisms are in place where the accuracy of district level reports can be ascertained. Again, return to bondage of previously released bonded labourers is neither recorded nor studied by the government. The effectiveness of rehabilitation schemes is poor. Various non-government organizations feel that the relapse rate is very high. One of the reasons is the long delay between identification of bonded labourers and their dispersal for rehabilitation. There is also widespread corruption among the enforcing officials, who are accused of siphoning funds earmarked for rehabilitation purposes. There is lack of adequate enforcement staff; number of personnel deployed for enforcement of child and bonded labour laws is woefully inadequate. The eradication of bonded labour depends upon the commitment of the government to two imperatives—proper enforcement of the Bonded Labour Act and creation of meaningful alternatives for already bonded labourers. Apart from government initiatives, it is incumbent on non-governmental organizations to collaborate in this effort. Bonded labour is vast and pernicious and deserves to be combated on many fronts. The district level vigilance committees have not been formed in many districts and even those, where they have been formed have remained dormant and inactive.

Provisions in Chapter III of the Act extinguished all liabilities to pay the bonded debt. Every obligation of a bonded labourer to repay any bonded debt shall be deemed to have been extinguished, and if any property the possession of which was taken over by the creditor shall be restored to the persons from whom it has been seized. The Act provides for punishment for compelling any person to render bonded labour. It also provides for (a) punishment for advancement of bonded debt, (b) punishment for extracting bonded labour, (c) punishment for omission to restore, possession of property of the bonded labourers. It provides for appointment for executive magistrates to try all such cases and vesting them with powers of judicial magistrate to summary trial of all such offences. The law also bars jurisdiction of the civil courts in respect of any matter to which the provisions of the Act are applicable.

Section 13 of the Act provides for constitution of vigilance committees at district and sub-divisional levels for effective implementation of the Act. It has been observed that hitherto a very formal rigid and legalistic approach has been followed while releasing bonded labourers from the fetters of bondage. Every case of release of bonded labourers is tried by a formal process of trial by the executive magistrate, appointed by the state government and vested with the powers of a judicial magistrate u/s 21 of the Bonded Labour System Act. A bonded labourer, said the Supreme Court can never stand up to the rigidity and tyranny of the legal process due to his/her poverty. The only way out of this impasse would be adoption of a summary trial immediately on receipt of a report from the concerned agencies so that identification and release could be simultaneous. This could also be the only practical solution to the problem of securing faster release.

There have been instances, where a stand has been taken by the bureaucracy that a person may not be released from debt bondage and rehabilitated until and unless the bonded labour keeper has been convicted. This is contrary to the spirit of the judgment of the Supreme Court in Santhal Pragna Antyodaya Ashram vs State of Bihar (1987 supplementary) Supreme Court cases 141 where the apex court had clearly observed, *"implementation of the rehabilitation programme should not wait on account of the pendency of the present preceding of the apex court"*. Any resistance from a bonded labour keeper to the release of the bonded labourer must, therefore, be struck down as ultra virus of the provisions of the Constitution and should not be allowed to stand in the way of release.

Magnitude of the Problem

In the absence of a National Household Survey (the first such survey was conducted by the Gandhi Peace Foundation in collaboration with the V.V. Giri National Labour Institute in 1978-79; but the findings were not acceptable to the government as the methodology adopted was considered to be not scientific. It is difficult to arrive at any definite conclusion about the total number of bonded labourers in the country. The survey stated that there are about 26.7 lakh bonded labourers in states surveyed by them. According to the information made available by state governments, there are about 2,86,000 bonded labourers identified through survey at the initial stage after the BLS (A) Act came into force. However, in the absence of information about the procedure adopted for the survey, it is not possible to authenticate the accuracy of such a figure. The identification of bonded labour is not even ten per cent of the conservative estimates of the bonded labour in the country.

Some of the problems encountered in the identification of the bonded labourers are:

- For fear of reprisals and loss of employment, the bonded labourers, mostly belonging to Scheduled Castes and Scheduled Tribes do not come forward to lodge any complaints against the perpetrators of the crime themselves.
- Aggressive environment created by the masters for maintenance of status quo in no way allows for filing of complaints.
- Malfunctioning of vigilance committees, lack of awareness on the part of local officials of the peculiarities and complexities of the bonded labour system.
- Paucity of voluntary agencies to identify bonded labourers and prevent cases of fraudulent identification.

UN Supplementary Convention on Abolition of Slavery 1956

Ground-Level Realities

In assessing the problem of the curse of bonded labour, some of the ground-level realities have to be kept in mind. There is an obvious attempt at denial and minimization of the problem. Many states take a stand that there are no bonded labourers in the state and all that was required to be done has been done. Though bonded labour is largely found in agricultural operations, it is also present in several other industries and occupations like brick kilns, rice mills, stone quarries, salt manufacturing works, leather tanning units, etc. Further, eradication of bonded labour is not a one-time event; it can occur and recur at any time, in any industry, or occupation. Unless the rehabilitation process is promptly completed, there is the danger of the released labourers relapsing into debt bondage again.

Contract and Migrant Bonded Labour

Problems of contract and migrant bonded labour are complex and sensitive. Their problem has become the subject-matter of several public interest litigations before the Hon'ble Supreme Court and High Courts. Bonded Labour System (Abolition) Act was amended in April, 1985 by adding an explanation to Section 2 and bringing contract and migrant labour within the purview of the Act, if such labourers come within the purview of the contract bonded labour system as defined in Section 2(g) of the Act. The modus operandi of recruitment of contracts of migrant labour are recruitment of labourers by the recruiting agents and bringing them to the work site, usually with family members, with alluring promises of good wages and better living conditions. But the promises are never kept and as soon as the workmen arrive at the work site, they are subjected to ruthless exploitation, long working hours and many other forms of exploitation. No wages are paid and the workmen continue to incur advances for their day-to-day biological survival.

Initiatives of the National Human Rights Commission

The Supreme Court in the Writ Petition No. 3922/1985—People's Union for Civil Liberties vs State of Tamil Nadu and Others—requested the NHRC to get involved in the monitoring of the implementation of the Bonded Labour System (Abolition) Act, 1976. Initiatives of NHRC involve the following:

(i) It focused attention on 13 states, namely, Andhra Pradesh, Arunachal Pradesh, Bihar, Haryana, Karnataka, Kerala, Madhya Pradesh, Maharashtra, Orissa, Rajasthan, Tamil Nadu and Uttar Pradesh, considered bonded labour prone by the Union Labour Ministry on the basis of several study reports.

(ii) Through special rapporteurs, it conducted reviews of the prevalence of bonded labour in the states and sent detailed reports to the concerned authorities. In the year 2000, the Commission constituted an expert group to recommend measures for the effective implementation of laws for the abolition of the bonded labour system. The group gave an action plan for NHRC and specified that the Commission should be involved in identification, release and rehabilitation of the bonded labour. One of the most important recommendations of the expert group was to incorporate in BLSA, through an appropriate amendment, a provision similar to Section 4 of Scheduled Caste and Scheduled Tribe (Prevention of Atrocities) Act, 1989, to deal with cases of wilful disregard of duties under the Act highlighted by the state-wise reviews. There has been no worthwhile follow up by the Commission.

(iii) A group was also constituted by the Commission to examine the incidence of witnesses turning hostile in cases against defaulting employers under the Act. The Commission also decided to obtain periodical information on prosecution of cases from the bonded labour-prone states. The Chairman of the Commission, Dr. A.S. Anand, in a letter to all the Chief Ministers dated September 12, 2006 pointed out the lack of initiative on the part of District Magistrates and Superintendents of Police in discharging their duties under provisions of the Act, resulting in many witnesses turning hostile due to coercion or threat by the accused persons.

(iv) The Commission also organized a national level workshop on elimination of bonded labour and child labour in June, 2007 and issued a number of guidelines for implementation by the state and central governments.

(v) Although the Commission has been stressing the importance of vigorous implementation of the Minimum Wages Act 1948, an interstate migrant worker men (Regulation of Employment and Conditions of Service) Act, 1979 in checking the evil of bonded labour, it has failed to take worthwhile steps to enforce its compliance.

NHRC organized another national seminar on September 30, 2011. Some of the salient recommendations of the national seminar were the following:

1. State governments should adopt Standing Operating Procedures (SOP) for developing a mechanism

through the labour department for registration of brick kilns and procedures for proper inspection by the enforcing agencies.

2. Provide training to the police and judiciary at the state and district level to sensitize them on the issue of bonded labour.
3. All pending cases filed under the Bonded Labour System (Abolition) Act, 1976, be disposed of immediately by taking recourse to summary trial and to issue release certificate in favour of those, who are found to be in bondage. The certificate should be handed over to the persons so released simultaneously in a language known to him or her.

Conclusion

Despite various initiatives of the National Human Rights Commission, the bonded labour system prevails in different forms. It is a curse and an outrage against humanity. The Supreme Court has taken cognizance of the issue on more than one occasion. It has given an expansive and liberal interpretation of the definition and issued a number of directions to the state and central governments on the subject. It has entrusted the responsibility of overseeing the extent of compliance with its directions to the National Human Rights Commission. However, elimination of bonded labour requires sustained, convergent and coordinated efforts by different stakeholders. Indeed, it has to be the concern of the whole nation. Unfortunately, political will is missing. District and state administration has to involve voluntary agencies in this endeavour. In the case of Neerja Chowdhury vs State of Madhya Pradesh (AIR 1984 Supreme Court 1099) the apex court visualized the important role of voluntary agencies in identifying rehabilitating bonded labour. The Court pinned its faith on the inclusion of members of voluntary groups in the vigilance committees. However, there is the danger that vested interests can easily have their own men selected as members of the vigilance committees by setting up dummy voluntary groups. The court also said that officers, who are posted at different levels to deal with the problem of the bonded labour system should be properly trained and sensitized so that they may develop a sense of involvement with the misery and sufferings of the poor.

A number of strategies have to be adopted. A compassionate, considerate and caring civil society has to take energetic steps to put an end to this curse. In the end, one can only say that democratic movements are the only way to counter social ills. Any number of laws and their interpretations can be made infructuous by the vested interests. Hence, a strong social democratic movement is called for to end this curse.

9

Child Labour and Child Marriage

Child Labour

Child labour has been defined as any work within or outside the family that involves time, energy and which affects the ability of the child to participate in leisure, play and educational activities. Such work goes to impair the health and development of the child. According to the International Labour Organization (ILO), child labour includes children working long hours for low wages under uncongenial conditions affecting their physical and mental development. Such children are also deprived of meaningful training and educational opportunities that would offer them a better future.

Definition of Child

Article 1 of the United Nations Convention on the Rights of the Child, (1990) defines a child as anyone below the age of 18 years. The Child Labour (Prohibition) and Regulation Act, 1986, defines a child "as a person who has not completed his 14th year of age". It can be mentioned in this connection that in India there is not one clear definition of the child. The legal definition varies with the specific legislation. The census of India speaks of persons below the age of 14 as children.

Most of these children work for long hours for a pittance in extremely miserable, exploitative and unsanitary conditions. In the agricultural sector also, with the consolidation of land holdings and mechanized farming, many people work on daily wages on other people's lands. It is common for adults in the rural areas to be hired on condition that the children also accompany them and work for the same long hours.

Indian Constitution

The Indian Constitution provides an impressive set of rights for children, some of which are not available even to the adults. Article 23(1) prohibits trafficking in human beings and forced labour. Article 24 of the Constitution prohibits employment of children below the age of 14 years in any factory, mines or hazardous activity. There are provisions in Part IV of the Constitution dealing with child rights. Article 39 of the Constitution lays down that children should be given opportunities and facilities to develop in a healthy manner and in conditions of freedom and dignity and that "childhood and youth should be protected against moral and material abandonment". Article 45 of the Constitution clearly lays down that the state shall endeavour to provide "within a period of 10 years from the commencement of the Constitution free and compulsory education for all children until they complete the age of 14 years". Article 37 of the Constitution, which makes the Directive Principles non-enforceable, also stipulates in unequivocal terms that these principles are "fundamental in the governance of the country and it shall be the duty of the state to apply these principles in making laws". Article 51(a)(k) on Fundamental Duties states that it shall be the duty of every citizen of

India who is a parent or guardian to provide opportunities for education to his child or, as the case may be, the ward between the age of 6 and 14 years.

International Safeguards

India became a party to the Convention on the Rights of the Child (1990) on December 11, 1992. The Convention reflects the concern of the international community for the protection of the rights of the children in all spheres. In the words of the Convention "in all actions concerning children the best interest of the child shall be a primary concern". The Convention lays down that "the child by reason of his physical and mental immaturity needs special safeguards and care including appropriate legal protection before as well as after birth. As a signatory to the Convention, India is under an obligation to take necessary legislative, administrative, social and educational measures to ensure implementation of the Convention. India has also ratified six ILO (International Labour Organization) Conventions relating to child labour. The ILO through its international programme on the Elimination of Child Labour (IPECL) has been playing an important role in the process of elimination of child labour and protection of children from various exploitative purposes. In June 1999, the Convention on the Worst Forms of Child Labour addressed issues such as rehabilitation as well as social integration of child labourers.

Magnitude of the Problem

The 2001 National Census estimated the number of working children at 12.6 million, out of a total of 200 million children aged between 5 to 14 years of whom 5.77 million were classified as "main workers" (those who have worked for six months preceding the date of enumeration) and 6.88 as marginal workers (those who had not worked for 183 days but have done some work). The number as per the 1991 census was 11.3 million. An analysis of 2001 data shows that the majority of main workers are boys, whereas the majority of marginal workers are girls. Many of the children are engaged in employment called hazardous labour, i.e. harmful to the physical, mental and moral well-being of the children.

Most of the child labourers belong to Scheduled Castes and other vulnerable sections. They are recruited for reducing the cost of production and their inherent incapacity to form unions to bargain for higher wages and improved working conditions. This explains the paradox of having a large pool of child labour amidst the high level of adult unemployment. Child labourers are recruited from poverty-stricken areas and areas that have suffered from natural calamities. Many children are also trafficked from these areas for exploitation as child labourers. Of late, many of them are engaged in quarries, construction industries, brick kilns, etc.

But children who should be in school but are out of school are deemed to be actual or potential child labourers. In rural India a child who does not go to a formal school is a working child because he/she performs various odd activities like collection of fuel, water, and miscellaneous domestic chores. It has to be borne in mind that in the rural sector the concept of a non-working and non-school going child does not exist.

Child labour is used in a big way not in the government but in various private enterprises. There are parts of the Indian economy, where children do not work at all. The Factory Acts ban employment of children in large factories. Paradoxically, in these industries, the wages are much better and higher. Specific sectors and areas where employment of children is very high include the match industry in

Shivakashi, glass industry in Ferozabad, brassware industry in Moradabad, carpet industry in Mirzapur, Jammu and Kashmir, lock-making industry in Aligarh and slate-making industry in Mandasaur. Thus, the Dickensian world of child labour is spread all over India and not confined to one region.

Causes of Child Labour

Causes of child labour are many and they emanate from the vicious cycle of poverty, unemployment and low wages. Unequal distribution of resources, lop-sided economic development and backward nature of agriculture are also contributory factors. Another main reason behind the widespread prevalence of child labour in India is the fact that primary education is not compulsory. Children out of school perform odd duties for long hours under sub-human conditions at poor wages. Parents of most of these children are poor, and deprived of basic education find it difficult to send their children to schools. Thus, as the children do not go to schools, it is not possible for them to break out of the illiteracy trap. It is a fact that, as pointed out by Myron Weiner, that the Indian government spends less on primary education than most other Asian countries and puts a disproportionate share of its educational resources on higher education, a political decision which benefited the middle classes, while leaving the rural and urban poor educationally impoverished[1]. Another important factor is the large family size, often the corollary of poverty and illiteracy. In families with many children, parents feel compelled to send one or more of the children to work since they cannot afford to send all the children to schools. The situation puts the girls in a disadvantageous position. Very often, to allow the brothers to go to schools, they are sent to work. Indeed, child labour has kept girls out of school. Employers are over-eager to employ girls since they are paid less than boys. In Shivakashi match factories, most of the girls are below the age of 14. The result is that female attendance in the primary schools is low and this explains the lower literacy of the females.

Actually poverty is not, as has been pointed out by a perceptive observer, the cause but often the consequence of child labour. Child labour perpetuates poverty on a large scale as several children lacking in skills grow up as unskilled workers with large families and then ask their children to follow the same benighted course. Again, child labour is spread in India and many South Asian countries because employers find it inexpensive and extremely lucrative. Children work for long hours with low wages and are more docile and easier to manage than adults. In a survey of carpet–weaving shop owners of Pakistan by Susan Crawford[2] it is mentioned that the majority of owners admitted that the availability of child labour in the area was the main reason for selection of a particular area to start business. They hire children as labourers because they work for longer hours with lower wages and are generally more obedient. They further feel that they are doing a good turn to the children, who would not in any way get an opportunity for education, by providing them money which their families need.

Supreme Court's Guidelines to Eliminate Child Labour

The Supreme Court in the case of M.C. Mehta vs State of Tamil Nadu (AIR 1997, SC 699) has laid down some useful guidelines for elimination of child labour. Some of them are: (1) Withdrawal of children working in hazardous industries and providing them education in appropriate institutions. (2) Identification of working children. (3) The defaulting employer should be asked to pay compensation of Rs. 20,000 for every child employed in contravention of law. The liability of the employers would not cease even when he disengages the child employed. (4) The sum, thus, collected will be put in a fund to be known as the Child Labour Rehabilitation Welfare Fund. It will be used to help the child to generate greater income. The state should also provide a job to an adult member of the family whose child was engaged in a hazardous industry.

NHRC's Initiatives

The National Human Rights Commission in its Annual Report (1994-95) emphasized the fact that it is not the absence of law or treaties that is responsible for persistence of child labour. A number of legislations already exist for prohibition and regulation of child labour. Apart from laws, like the Factory Act 1948, Mines Act 1952, Bidi and Cigar Workers (Conditions of Employment) Act 1976, child labour is prohibited in scheduled occupations and processes under the Child Labour (Prohibition and Regulation) Act 1986. In the Memorandum of Action taken on the annual report of the NHRC, the Ministry of Home Affairs[3] mentioned that the government is examining a number of suggestions with a view to adding more teeth to the Child Labour Act. The Commission in its Annual Report (1995-96), expressed the unequivocal view that the problem of child labour will persist till compulsory education for all up to the age of 14 is realized. The then Chairperson of the Commission addressed a letter to the Presidents of all major political parties in India and observed that, despite the provision of Article 45 of the Indian Constitution, the grim reality is that today the number of illiterates in the country exceeds the entire population of the country at the time of independence. This grotesque reality enfeebles the country in every way and affects the dignity and self-esteem of countless Indians and exposes them to outrageous human rights violations. The Chairperson urged that definite steps should be taken to translate into legislation the Directive Principles contained in Article 45 of the Constitution. It is due to the Commission's continued and unceasing efforts that education has become a fundamental right for the children between the age group of 6 to 14 years through the 86th amendment of the Constitution.

At the request of the Commission, Prof. R.K. Mishra of Banaras Hindu University conducted a survey of child labour in the sari industry of Banaras. The portrait of the child worker emerging from the report is very depressing. Thousands of children from the poor Ansari (weaving community families) are drawn at the sari industry at the age of 6 or 7 and are made to work for long hours in unhealthy and poorly ventilated rooms without rest or leisure. There is no concept of leave or weekly off. The wages are abysmally low. Sometimes parents take an advance (from Rs. 2,000 to 5,000) from the employers for the services of the children. According to the established usage the services cannot be withdrawn until the advance is paid up by the parents. This tradition and mindset has been passed on from generation to generation and the children remain without education and have no future except weaving.

Investigation and sight visits to illegal coal mines in the Jayantiya Hills area of Meghalaya showed that a large number of child labourers were forced to work under miserable conditions and lead lives worse than those of animals. They crawl into excavated spaces through small holes and extract coal in wooden carts small enough to fit through the holes. These places are called "rat mines" and the rat miners are brought from Nepal, Bangladesh and some Indian states. About 70,000 children were found engaged in this kind of labour. (Alternative country report and update on India—3rd and 4th combined periodic reports on the Convention on the Rights of Children 2002 and 2003)

The Commission has constantly monitored the child labour situation in the country through its special rapporteurs and through various sensitization projects. It has coordinated with state governments and NGOs in combating the problem of child labour. It specially monitored child labour in carpet belts areas in UP, the bangle glass industry in Ferozabad and silk industry in Karnataka.

The Commission has persistently questioned the absurd distinction of hazardous and non-hazardous child labour. It has held the clear view that hazardous should be considered in relation to the child and not the industry or the occupation. It has strongly urged that all child labour should fall in the hazardous category and should, therefore, be banned.

In 1996-97 the Commission received some disturbing reports on employment of children below the age of 14 years as domestic servants in the homes of government officials. It took up the matter with the central government and state governments to amend the Civil Services Conduct Rules 1964, prohibiting such employment. The conduct rules have been amended by the central government and all state governments. Now employment of children below the age of 14 years as domestic servants by government employees is regarded as a misconduct inviting a major penalty.

The Commission has used the services of special rapporteurs to monitor the incidence of child labour in different states and from time to time issued directives to different states in respect of detection and withdrawal of children engaged in hazardous occupations and admission of such children into the formal and non-formal system of schooling. It has also tried to ensure economic rehabilitation of the affected families and prosecution of offending employers. In a letter (April 9, 2001) to the state governments, the Commission referred to complaints regarding prevalence of child labour in the slaughter houses all over India. It urged the state government to stop this malevolent practice and prosecute the owners violating the law and get the children released.

The problem of child labour is complex and gargantuan. In the Annual Report (2005-06) the Commission admits that it has no hesitation in admitting that "its achievements are disproportionally small compared with the magnitude of the problem. Child labour persists in most of the states in India despite several pronouncements of the Supreme Court and sincere efforts of social action groups and activists...... and...now that free and elementary education has been made a fundamental right of every child up to the age of 14 years, the Commission hopes that all state governments will ensure cent per cent enrolment and retention of all school going children, which alone can provide a lasting solution to the problem of child labour". The scourge of child labour haunts the country. Elimination of child labour is relevant to Millennium Development Goals like ensuring that all boys and girls complete primary schooling (MDG 2).

Child Marriage

Child marriage in India is an age-old social evil that has a long history. Various factors such as social, cultural and economic are responsible for the growth of this baneful custom. In the past, it had its origin from the need to protect unmarried girls from the eyes of the foreign invaders. Later on, it became a rigid social custom. The problem has been further compounded by the dowry system. Fears of payment of heavy dowry for the marriage of a girl after puberty made the practice common, particularly, among the poor and economically weaker sections of the society. In the rural areas, in some states, if the girl is not married before she has attained the age of seventeen years, the entire family is ostracized.

It is aptly said that child marriage is an evil "greater than Sati because it is far more devastating in its consequences and more insidious in its working." For the girl, it leads to inadequate socialization, discontinuation of education, great physiological and psychological damages owing to repeated pregnancies. There is evidence to show that the maximum maternal deaths take place between fifteen to sixteen years of age when a girl is no longer a child and yet unprepared for marriage.

Under the Child Marriage Restraint Act (after its amendment in 1978), the minimum legal marriage age in India is eighteen years for women and twenty-one years for men. The Social Development Council, New Delhi conducted a study of child marriages in Rajasthan and Andhra Pradesh and concluded that this piece of legislation has remained a dead letter because of the prevalent social and religious customs, poor economic conditions and very ineffective enforcement machinery. Although the prescribed age limit for the marriage of girls is eighteen years, hundreds of girls are married on the occasion of Akashya Tritiya in Rajasthan as well as in some parts of Bihar, Andhra Pradesh and Tamil Nadu.

The widespread prevalence of child marriage in certain parts of the country has been of great concern to the National Human Rights Commission. In its Annual Report (1995-96), the NHRC endorsed the Draft Marriage Bill proposed by the National Commission for Women and the Department of Women and Child Development intending to replace the Child Marriage Restraint Act of 1929. The central government in its Action Taken Report of that year, did not accept the recommendations of NHRC and took the view that major social and economic efforts are required to bring an end to the practice of child marriage among those sections of society and community, where such marriages are being conducted for a long time. The Commission in its Annual Report (1997-97), expressed the strong view that the response of the central government and the 'Memorandum of Action Taken' amounted to a total disinclination to strengthen and alter the law, or indeed to ensure its better implementation, in any manner, in respect of these very important social and cultural problems. The Commission further stated that the responsibility of the central government did not cease because the present Act was administered by the state government, or the issue of Personal Law should be advanced to block any effort, whatsoever, in this matter[4].

Meanwhile, after publication of a news item in an English daily that the child marriage on a large scale will be solemnized in Rajasthan on April 29, 1998, the day of Akashya Tritiya, the National Human Rights Commission issued a notice to the Chief Secretary of Rajasthan and called for a detailed report. It wanted to know the action taken on the part of the state government to prevent child marriages. It also detailed a team for an on-the-spot probe. Senior officers of the Commission visited Bikaner and Jodhpur and witnessed a number of child marriages being solemnized with great fanfare and without any restriction from the authorities and members of the public. The Commission had to point out to the state government that it is a statutory obligation on its part under the Child Marriage Restraint Act to prevent child marriages and for taking appropriate proceedings in accordance with the provisions of the Act. The National Human Rights Commission also called for a report from the Government of Rajasthan on the prevalence of child marriages in the state. The state government in its reply mentioned the steps it had taken to create social awareness against this longstanding evil. In its reply, the state government observed that the Health Department, Department of Women & Child Welfare had been organizing meetings and seminars, publishing advertisements in newspapers, distributing handbills to sensitize people about the evils of child marriage and the statutory provisions prohibiting the same. Earlier, the High Court of Rajasthan, in a civil writ petition (the case of Sushilla Ghoshala vs State of Rajasthan) expressed great concern at the continuance of child marriages in the state in spite of the Child Marriage Restraint Act, which is in force in the state. The High Court also stated that apart from educating the people against child marriage through meetings and seminars at the village level, the provisions of the Act should be made more stringent with deterrent punishment for the contraveners. Child Marriage Prevention Officers should be appointed as provided in the Act to prevent child marriages being performed in contravention of the provisions of the Act and for effective prosecution of the person violating the Act.

The Commission also undertook a study of the Child Marriage Restraint Act. It carefully examined the provisions of the Act and felt that some amendments of the Act were called for. For example, Sections 3 and 5 of the Act provide inadequate punishment and fine on a person, who performs or conducts a child marriage. As the offences under the Act are not cognizable, no arrest can be made without an order or the judicial magistrate. This causes delay and fails to provide the desired deterrent effect. The National Human Rights Commission felt that the Act has to be amended to make the offence cognizable, non-bailable and triable in the Sessions Court. However, there should be greater emphasis on the prevention of child marriages, rather than bare annulment. The procedures for prosecution under the Act are cumbersome and penalty is not deterrent enough. Further, public participation in the implementation of the Act was poor.

In December 1999, the NHRC considered the question whether it would be preferable to provide for compulsory registration of marriages in the Hindu Marriage Act 1955 through appropriate amendments instead of making such a provision in the Child Marriage Restraint Act (CMRA). After considering the whole issue, the Commission decided to review the CMRA and recommended to the Government of India, a number of amendments to it. In pursuance of these amendments, the Government of India introduced the Prevention of Child Marriage Bill in the Rajya Sabha. The proposed bill had now been passed by both Houses of Parliament. It got the assent of the President of India on January 10, 2007, and is known by the nomenclature "The Prohibition of Child Marriage Act 2006" (No. 6 of 2007). The Commission had written to the state governments and all the other concerned agencies to organize mass-scale awareness programmes/campaigns. Some of the state governments also reported to the Commission the action taken by them. There were some unfortunate episodes also in the course of these campaigns. The government of Madhya Pradesh reported that in order to bring the state to "zero child marriage level" it has undertaken intense and coordinated awareness campaigns. All the Aanganwadi workers engaged in Integrated Child Development Skill (ICDS) were involved in preventing child marriages. However, there was a horrible incident in Dhar district of MP in which both hands of Shakuntala Verma, an ICDS supervisor, were chopped off when she tried to prevent organization of mass child marriages and launched a mass awareness campaign against such marriages.

Missing Children

The National Human Rights Commission has expressed concern regarding problems of missing children and in many cases sought reports from state governments. But after serial killings of small children in Nithari in NOIDA, there was shock and revulsion all over the country. Nithari killings highlighted the problems of missing children.

Data on missing children, placed in Parliament in 2014 showed that over 3.25 lakh children were missing between 2011 to 2014 (till June 2014) at the average rate of about 1 lakh children going missing every year. Fifty-five per cent of those missing were girls and 45 per cent of all missing children had remained untraced. Maharashtra is one of the worst states in terms of missing children with about 50,000 having disappeared between 2011 to 2014.

The police unfortunately seldom investigate cases of missing children. Under the existing arrangements, no serious efforts are really made to trace missing children and this constitutes a major loophole in our existing arrangements of prevention and control of crimes against children.

On February 12, 2007, the National Human Rights Commission constituted a committee to thoroughly examine the issue of missing children and give its suggestions so that appropriate guidelines may be evolved by the Commission and forwarded to the concerned authorities across states, union territories as well as to the Government of India. The committee set up by the NHRC under one of its members P.C. Sharma made a number of recommendations that would facilitate tracing and restoring of children to their families as well as support systems where they could be taken care of and protected. It contains a bold suggestion that preliminary enquiries into cases of missing persons could be outsourced by the police to NGOs, who are willing to undertake the task. Such NGOs can be notified by the state government. MHA may also issue separate guidelines to the NGOs. Synergy between the law enforcement agencies and the NGOs would be of great help and use in this regard. In the words of the NHRC Committee, missing children constitute a veritable "black hole in law enforcement". Unfortunately, state police authorities have so far failed to acknowledge the gravity of the problem and steps to carry out recovery of missing children remain a matter of low priority.

The Supreme Court had pulled up the central government for displaying insensitivity towards protection of child rights and inability to set up an advisory board under the Juvenile Justice Act. The Centre had also failed to inform the court on how many children were traced in 2014 (*Times of India*, April 17, 2015).

Notes

1. Myron Weiner, *The Child and the State of India.*
2. Susan Crawford. *Child Labour in South East Asia.*
3. Ministry reference to Child Marriage, Annual Report 1996-97, p. 118.
4. National Human Rights Commission Annual Report 1996-97, Para 4.8.

10
Handling of Complaints

One of the key functions of the National Human Rights Commission is to enquire into the complaints of human rights violations by the public servants through their acts of commission, omission and negligence. Speedy enquiry into the complaints by the Commission followed by clear recommendations enhances the credibility of the Commission in the public mind. The Protection of the Human Rights Act (PHRA) has given a wide mandate to the Commission. Section 12 of the PHRA lays down the following functions of the Commission.

1. Inquire suo motu or on a petition presented to it by a victim or any person on his behalf or on a direction or order of any court, into the complaint of (i) violation of human rights or abetment thereof; or (ii) negligence in the prevention of such violation, by a public servant.
2. Intervene in any proceeding involving any allegation of violation of human rights pending before a court, with the approval of such a court.
3. Visit, notwithstanding anything contained in any other law for the time being in force, any jail or other institution under the control of the state government, where persons are detained or lodged for purposes

of treatment, reformation or protection, for the study of the living conditions of inmates thereof and make recommendations thereon to the government.

4. Review the safeguards provided by or under the Constitution or any law for the time being in force for the protection of human rights and recommend measures for their effective implementation.
5. Review the factors, including acts of terrorism that inhibit the enjoyment of human rights and recommend appropriate remedial measures.
6. Study treaties and other international instruments on human rights and make recommendations for their effective implementation.
7. Undertake and promote research in the field of human rights.
8. Spread human rights literacy among various sections of society and promote awareness about the safeguards available for the protection of these rights through publications, the media, seminars and other available means.
9. Encourage the efforts of non-governmental organizations and institutions working in the field of human rights.
10. Such other functions, as it may consider necessary, for the protection of human rights.

Indeed, for any human rights institution, complaints handling mechanism is of great importance and a critical tool for its efficient functioning. This is particularly so in case of India, where court proceedings are time- consuming and very often inaccessible to those, whose rights have been violated. Unless a complaint handling mechanism functions effectively, the Commission will find it difficult to discharge its functions efficiently and its credibility will be dented.

The complaints before the Commission, include, cases of alleged custodial death, torture, police highhandedness, violations committed by security forces, prison conditions, atrocities on women and children, bonded labour, negligence by public authority, etc. The number of complaints received by the Commission has grown exponentially from the low figure of 169 in 1993-94 to 106,990 in 2012-13. The annual average, has thus, shot up from 15,352 in the first five years (1993-94 to 1997-98) to 91,616 in 2008-09 to 2012-13. The case load has now stabilized around 100,000. This speaks of the growing credibility of the Commission and the yearning of the people for trouble-free expeditious justice.[1]

Complaints received during the last five years (2008-09 to 2012-13) show that the following states, namely, Haryana, Uttar Pradesh, Bihar, Rajasthan, Delhi, and Maharashtra account for nearly 78 per cent of the total complaints. The largest number of complaints are being received from Uttar Pradesh followed by Delhi. Complaints received from southern and north-eastern states are somewhat low, particularly from north-eastern states, where counter-insurgency operations are afoot. It is clear that the Commission is not being equally accessed by different parts of the country.

The skewed regional distribution has persisted since the inception of the Commission. Though NHRC does not give reasons for the pattern, it is reasonable to assume that the physical proximity to the Commission whose headquarters are in New Delhi, linguistic similarity, poor administrative culture in some of the states reporting a high number of complaints could be some of the reasons behind this phenomenon. The Commission has not so far been able to open its regional offices in South India and in the North-East, though its mandate allows it to do so.

In Limini Disposal

Analysis of disposal of complaints by the Commission shows that a large number of cases have been dismissed in limini by the Commission for lack of jurisdiction or on other grounds of rejection. During the period between October 1993 to March 31, 2013, 54 per cent of total numbers of complaints have been dismissed in limini. It is also seen that disposal in limini has come down from 79.78 per cent in the first ten years, 1993-94 to 2002-03 to 42.98 per cent in the second ten years 2003-04 to 2012-13.[2] Disposal of a large number of cases in limini is disheartening and disappointing to the complainants. It is true that many of the complaints received by the Commission do not fall within the jurisdiction of the Commission, but unless a very transparent procedure is adopted, disposal of many cases in limini will continue to upset the complainants. Reasons for disposal in limini of the complaints should be clearly indicated and explained to the complainants.

It seems that the NHRC has become the victim of its own formalism. Gearty Conor has aptly said, "that it is a risky venture in any society, even a democratic one to put the judges in the front line of human rights protection. The second risk is an even a greater one. An over-commitment to the legalism of human rights drains the subject of life, emptying much of its ethical activism and moral energy and replacing these vital forces with the careful accuracy and the passionless pedantry of the law."[3] Ideally, the complaint mechanism of any National Human Rights Institution (NHRI) should be free of jargon and devoid of bureaucratic impediments, with simplified procedures. This is the best method of ensuring accessibility to the most vulnerable sections of the society.

At the instance of the Commission, the well-known management firm McKinsey, produced a report on expeditious handling of the pending complaints before the Commission. The report pointed out that the Commission's grievance redressal function will be affected as the time taken for grievance redressal extends. Further, other functions assigned to the Commission will also be affected because the members will not have the time to pursue them vigorously.

McKinsey recommended a three-step solution (1) In the short term, add qualified people in a few critical areas to increase processing capacity and bring in new management systems and processes to improve efficiency. (2) In the longer term, consider ways, in which case load can be segmented to cut the inflow of work while maintaining a high degree of impact. (3) On a certain date, split the Commission into a "new Commission" and an "old Commission" with the old Commission processing old cases and the new Commission dealing with the fresh cases. Another suggestion was for the NHRC to delegate all but the most pressing complaints to the state commissions and for NHRC to send cases concerning police work to the relevant authorities to investigate, take action and report back to the NHRC within a month.

Complaints Against the Police

Complaints against the police form the bulk of the total number of complaints received by the Commission. They averaged around 40 per cent in the first ten years of the Commission. In the year 2011-12 the police accounted for 36 per cent of the total number of complaints. The figure dropped to 33 per cent during the year 2012-13, the drop in the percentage of the number of complaints is perhaps due to the growing sensitization of the police and increase of complaints against other categories of public servants. The complaints against the defence forces, including, the para-military forces barely constitute 1 per cent of the total number of complaints. This possibly is due to the perception in the public mind that the Commission exercises limited control and jurisdiction over the armed forces.

The proportion of petitions in which the allegation has been proved and relief recommended by the Commission is less than half of the total number of complaints taken up for enquiry by the Commission. The proportion of cases in which allegations were not substantiated was 56 per cent (4,432 out of a total of 7,825) and 60 per cent (4,093 out of a total of 6,700) during 2010-11 and 2011-12 respectively).

Suo Moto Cognizance

It is unfortunate that the Commission has not taken suo moto cognizance of many cases. It is less than 1 per cent of the cases registered during the period from 2008-09 to 2012-13 (ibid). Suo moto cognizance of important cases enables the Commission to play a positive and a proactive role.

The Commission has taken some positive measures to improve the handling of the case load as early as in 1997-1998. It had done a management study to ensure better management of the case load.

For better and quicker and more satisfying disposal of cases the following measures can be useful.

1. The Commission has to ensure that its online data base is up-to-date and accurate. Sometimes information available to the complainants do not match the information available with the Commission. According to the office of the UN High Commissioner for Human Rights, "National Institutions should ensure the availability of information materials in appropriate languages, which set out the procedure for lodging complaints in clear terms". The Commonwealth Secretariat's *Best Practice for National Human Rights*

Institutions also points out that NHRIs should aim at providing information and documentation not only in the dominant language spoken in the country but in other languages as well.[4]

2. Create a specially trained small unit for screening the admissibility of cases at the preliminary stage.
3. Ensure that the Commission's Practice Directions and Procedures Regulations with regard to complaints are adhered to by all members of the staff.
4. Victim-centred responsive and problem solving approach to complaints instead of an overly legalistic one has to be adopted.
5. Ensure that information in the online case database is accurate and up-to-date. It may be mentioned in this connection that the Australian Human Rights Commission, for example, undertakes great efforts to be transparent and accountable. Details of the complaint processes are clearly outlined on the website and deadlines and time limits are provided. The institution has also a so-called service charter which provides a way through which users can understand the nature and standard of service they can expect and how they can contribute to service improvement.
6. Inform the complainants regularly of the scope, timing and progress of the proceedings and the disposition of their cases.
7. Allow for decisions made by the Commission to appeal against and set up an appropriate review appeals mechanism.
8. All the staff of the NHRC must receive training after joining the Commission.

9. Regional offices are necessary for the widespread accessibility of the Commission. It will help the Commission to promptly reach out to the complaints received from different corners of the country.

Investigation

The Commission has an investigation wing of its own headed by an officer of the rank of Director General of Police. It carries out investigations into various complaints received by the Commission. The Ministry of Home Affairs which is the nodal Ministry of NHRC, unfortunately, was initially of the opinion that a skeleton investigation wing would serve the needs of the Commission. It held the untenable view that the Commission on its own would not have to take up investigation of many cases and hence may not require a full-fledged investigation wing. Further it could always, as provided u/s 14 of the PHRA, use the services of any officer or investigation agency of the state or central government. As the first Director General of the Investigation Wing, I could convince the Commission that it would soon be inundated with complaints and it must have a well organized investigation wing with adequate staff to get to grips with the situation. It would be unbecoming of the Commission to depend on the investigation wings of other agencies for its work. After initial hiccups, the government, despite many queries and objections, ultimately sanctioned the staff for the Commission. It was mainly due to the first Chairman Justice Shri R.N. Misra's firm intervention, the bureaucratic hurdles collapsed and our original proposal with minor alterations was accepted.

The following comparative statement gives an indication of the case load of the investigation wing of the Commission.

Investigation	*Total*	*Annual Average (April 2003-March 2014)*	*Annual Average (April 2003-March 2014)*
Custodial death cases	6,693	29	626
Spot enquiries	817	83 (Data available for 3 years 2000-01 to 2002-03)	55
Fact finding cases	27,764	953	1,825
Rapid action cases (introduced from 2007-08)	1,488 Annual average: 238		

Many NGO groups initially felt that in the investigation wing, there should not only be police officers or ex-police officers but also investigators with different backgrounds such as academics, lawyers, etc. who cannot be charged with pro-police sympathies. In principle, this was unexceptionable. However, in practice it was very difficult to get lawyers or academics in the pool of the investigators. No one was willing to come either on deputation or join permanently in the NHRC because of the low pay scale of the government. Later on, during investigation of specific cases, the Commission was able to enlist valuable help from some of the NGO groups. The civil society groups also felt that the Commission was not doing justice to the complainants by referring their petitions in many cases to the very police, who are primarily responsible for violation of their human rights. It is necessary perhaps for the Commission to have a close hard look into this issue. It is a fact that the Commission, as a routine, measure forwards the complaints to the concerned authorities, who are very often the perpetrators themselves without adopting the practice that if a complainant requests anonymity the request must be respected with a view to ensuring his/her safety, security and dignity. The Asian Centre for Human Rights has correctly pointed out that this routine practice exposes the complainants to the danger of retaliatory measures from the authorities against whom they have complained.[5]

Custodial Violence

Custodial violence, and particularly, death in police custody has been one of the key concerns of the Commission since its inception. Custodial violence, and particularly custodial death, does irretrievable damage to the image of the police and sullies its reputation. In the words of the Supreme Court, "custodial violence is a calculated assault on human dignity and whenever human dignity is wounded civilization takes a step backward. The flag of humanity on each occasion must fly half mast." (D.K. Basu vs State of West Bengal).

The National Human Rights Commission immediately after its formation in 1993, issued directions to the District Magistrates and Superintendents of Police in all states in the country to report within 24 hours all cases of custodial death and custodial rape, failing which an adverse inference of "cover-up" would be drawn by the Commission. At the same time, the NHRC also felt concerned at the uneven quality of post-mortem reports. In a number of instances, it came to the Commission's notice that post-mortem reports appeared to have been doctored due to the influence of officials, who perpetrated the offence. There was also an inordinate delay in writing of the post-mortem reports. In cases of custodial death, very often the fate of cases depends upon the opinion given by the doctors in post-mortem reports. There can be total miscarriage of justice if the reports are manipulated and the doctors intimidated. The Commission, therefore, recommended video-filming of post-mortem examinations and sending tapes to the Commission for scrutiny with a view to preventing malpractices. The Commission also circulated for adoption a model autopsy form that took into consideration the work done by the United Nations on the subject and special circumstances prevailing in the country. The instructions of the Commission had the desired effect of ensuring timely intimation to the Commission of deaths in police and jail custody from all states.

1. A total of 2,860 custodial deaths in police custody (PCD) and 21,964 in judicial custody (JCD) have been reported by various states since the Commission's inception in October, 1993 to March, 2013. It gives an annual average of 147 police and 1,126 judicial deaths. The comparative figures for the period October, 1993 to March, 2003 (first decennial) and April, 2003 to March, 2013 (second decennial) are 151 and 143 police and 747 and 1,487 jail deaths respectively.[6]

In this connection, it may be pointed out that though every case of custodial death is not due to the violation of human rights and many reports received from state authorities are closed by the Commission without ordering any monetary relief. The Commission's annual reports mention the number of deaths in police and jail custody without taking the outcome of detailed examination into consideration. In this respect, it seems that Commission's reporting of incidence of custodial death is somewhat flawed, as it gives an exaggerated picture which is quoted by the press and civil society groups. It will be more appropriate if the number of custodial deaths reported to the Commission and the number of cases on completion of enquiries reveal violation or negligence in prevention of human rights comes to notice are mentioned separately. This will also reduce the variation in the figures of deaths in police or jail custody reported by the Commission and the National Crimes Records Bureau.[7]

Compensation

Monetary compensation is recommended for victims' families in all cases of custodial deaths when the investigation discloses violation of human rights or negligence in prevention of such violation. The original Act empowered the Commission to recommend interim relief to the complainant on completion of the enquiry. The 2006 amendment (Section 18(C)) enables the Commission to recommend immediate relief to the victim at any stage of enquiry. The Commission has granted compensation to the victims in many cases. It has recommended and ensured payment of compensation to the tune of Rs. 70,41,53,500 in 3,214 cases involving 28 states and 5 Union Territories. In addition, Rs. 27,94,00,000 has been recommended for the victims' families in the Punjab Mass Cremation case in 2007-08. However, the Commission has not been able to get confirmation and details of payment of compensation to the next-of-kin of the identified victims ordered by it long ago.

In some cases, some of the state governments have taken the stand that compensation could be paid only when the officials accused of violation of human rights have been found guilty in the court of law. In one case of custodial death in Balia in UP of Atal Bihari Mishra, a student of Benaras Hindu University, the Commission pointed out to the state government that such a stand is incorrect and the award of interim relief u/s 18(3) by any state is not dependent on the establishment of the culpability of the public servant. "The remedy is independent of such petty-foggeries. Any state professing to be a welfare state should ensure a legal construction to promote the philosophy of the statute and advance its beneficial and benevolent purposes". The Commission said "the view that implies that administration of such interim relief could be at the end of the day after the guilt of the offending public servant is established in a criminal trial on the standards of criminal evidence would nullify the great humanism the statute seeks to enshrine. The Commission only hopes that the government of Uttar Pradesh is an ally of those values and will respond in a way which accords with the message and the philosophy of the law and its obligation as a "welfare state". The Government of Uttar Pradesh subsequently paid compensation to the victim's family as recommended by the Commission.

Visits to Police Lockups

Disturbed by increasing reports of violence in police lockups, the Commission decided that its officers will make surprise visits to police lockups. Section 12(c) of the Protection of Human Rights Act allows the Commission to visit jails and other places, where persons are detained or lodged for the purposes of treatment, reformation or protection, to study the living conditions of the inmates and make recommendations therein. The Secretary General of the Commission wrote to the Chief Secretaries of the States to issue necessary instructions to enable the officers of the NHRC to visit police lockups as well. A number of states accepted the suggestion. The Commission also issued detailed instructions to the officers regarding the manner in which they are to inspect the lockups. List of do's and don'ts were prepared and circulated among the NHRC officers. Unfortunately, there was strong police resistance to implement the proposal and NHRC also did not follow up the matter with vigour.

Human Rights Cells

The Commission had urged the police administration in the states to set up human rights cells in the police headquarters which will serve as links between the NHRC and the state police agencies. This body will also take steps to ensure human rights training and sensitization of police officers and men organized through workshops and seminars on human rights in association with the State Human Rights Commissions and the NHRC and actively promote human rights literacy and awareness. Unfortunately, the human rights cells in state police headquarters have not functioned effectively and efficiently. Civil society groups have also berated this failure on the part of NHRC. Very often, police officers, including senior police leaders, express fear that NHRC has become a police-bashing agency and the police have been singled out as the sole violator of human rights. This is a mistaken impression. NHRC does look into many cases of violation of human rights by other agencies of the government but violation by the police are invariably more serious and sinister because they deprive people of their lives and liberties and leave behind scars which take a long time to heal. For this it is necessary for the NHRC to carry the leadership of police with it, making it clear to the police personnel that the goal is not to punish but to ensure compliance with the rules and laws by the police. Willing compliance is to be preferred to exacting deterrence.

Notes

1. *Journal of NHRC 2012-13,* National Haman Rights Commission—Retrospective by Chaman Lal and Savita Bhakry, pp. 149-189.
2. Ibid.
3. Human Rights in the Age of Globalization—The "Challenge of Growing Up", a talk delivered on the occasion of Human Rights Day, December 10, 2002, LSE London.
4. National Human Rights Institutions—Best Practice", 2001 p. 9, Commonwealth Secretariat, London
5. India's NHRC "The best case is the worst, Asian Centre for Human Rights, (*ACHR Review,* September 15, 2004), p. 37.
6. *Journal of the National Human Rights Commission,* Vol. 12, 2013, National Human Rights Commission—A Retrospective by Chaman Lal and Savita Bhakhry.
7. Ibid.

11
Human Rights Education

The Preamble of the Universal Declaration of Human Rights, 1948, clearly states that recognition and respect for human rights is the foundation of freedom, peace and justice in the world. Denial of human rights is not only an individual or personal tragedy, but also creates conditions of social unrest, political turmoil and sows seeds of conflict between nations. However, proper implementation of human rights requires that everyone must know his or her rights. There is indeed a close relationship between legislation, implementation and education.

Article 26(2) of the Universal Declaration of Human Rights, states that, *"Education shall be directed to the full development of a human personality and to the strengthening of respect of human rights and fundamental freedoms. It shall promote understanding, tolerance and friendship among the nations, racial or religious groups and shall further the activities of the United Nations for the maintenance of peace"*. Only when people become aware of their rights can they ensure that their rights will not be trampled on and they will also develop respect for the rights of others.

The General Conference of the United Nations Educational, Scientific and Culture Organization (UNESCO), in its 18th session in Paris, 1974, recommended that education should be redirected for the full development of the human personality and to the strengthening of the respect for human rights and fundamental freedoms. *"It shall promote understanding and tolerance among all nations, racial or religious groups and shall further the activities of the United Nations for the sake of peace"*. The document further states that education shall help every person to understand and assume his or her responsibilities for the maintenance of peace. Indeed, UNESCO had played a very prominent and laudable role in the promotion of human rights education. The document *"plan of action by UNESCO further mentions though the cold war has come to an end and the walls have broken down, the last decade of the 20th century is witnessing the recurrence of most serious human rights violations caused by racism, xenophobia and religious intolerance"*.

The World Conference on Human Rights held at Vienna in 1993, reaffirmed that states are duty bound as stipulated in the Universal Declaration of Human Rights and the International Covenant on Economic, Social and Cultural Rights and in other international instruments to ensure that education promotes respect for human rights and fundamental freedoms. States must work out educational programmes that promote tolerance and foster peace and understanding among nations and different religious, social and ethnic groups.

Illiteracy Problem

However, the problem of illiteracy in many countries of Asia and Africa is very serious. Education in human rights cannot succeed to the fullest extent unless there is a satisfactory level of literacy. Article 45 of the Indian Constitution lays down that the state shall endeavour to provide within a period of 10 years from the commencement of the date of the Constitution free and compulsory education for children till they complete the age of 14 years.

Teaching of Human Rights

Human rights teaching must be conditioned by the values and the ethos of the society. In India, there is a wide-spread impression that human rights is a Western concept that has been imposed on us by Western powers. This is an erroneous impression. Since ancient days human rights in various forms have been the cultural heritage of mankind. In 1968, as a part of the contribution of the Human Rights year, the UNESCO brought out a publication entitled *The Birthright of Man,* which illustrates the concept of human rights from different cultural traditions and explains how the ideology of human rights is not exclusively Western in origin. In the final analysis says an American author, *"human rights is really about human dignity, a notion familiar to India's civilization centuries before the West was born[1]"*.

It is also desirable to teach human rights in terms of inter-individual or societal duties. If rights are explained in terms of duties, they are unlikely to be abused. Mahatma Gandhi laying stress on duty consciousness said, *"I learned from my illiterate and wise mother that all rights to be deserved and preserved come from duty well done. Thus, the very right to live, accrues to us when we do the duty of the citizenship of the world"*.

Teaching of human rights in the adult education programme should emphasize that violation of human rights are frequent and rampant because people are not active and vigilant. Denial of human rights even to one person shall be a matter of concern to the entire community. In developing countries of Asia, Africa and Latin America, there is massive violation of human rights of the disadvantaged groups and the marginalized sections of the society. In these societies, human rights education will have a transformative impact and will help in building a good society where basic rights and freedom of the people will be safeguarded.

Methodology

In devising methodology for teaching human rights it has to be kept in mind that an educational course will be effective if it is rooted in concrete situations faced by the students. Every curriculum should take into account real life issues and problems of the students concerned and suggest appropriate ways in dealing with them. Students should be encouraged to ponder over these issues and come up with suggestions. This interactive and participatory mode of training should become a part of the actual classroom pedagogy. Mere formal and theoretical instruction will not help in sensitizing the students.

For the success of the training programmes, the role of committed teachers is of utmost importance. Teachers are the pivots round which all education revolves. Any attempt to introduce human rights education in the school will not be successful unless teachers/educators are properly oriented. In the field of human rights, teachers' own perception of human rights and comments will count more than a well prepared curriculum and elaborate guidelines. Unfortunately, very little has been done to sensitize teachers on human rights issues. It has to be borne in mind that in the transference process about human rights teaching methods, which emphasize a hierarchical and authoritarian relationship between teachers and students has to be discouraged. This kind of transference will be self-defeating and distort the contents of the human rights. An interactive approach which allows learners to pause and think over the underlying principles of human rights and imbibe them and reflect them in work and conduct is the need of the day. In a paper titled "Education for Human Rights and Democracy", Dr. A.K. Sharma, former Director NCERT, mentioned that there have been instances where teachers have expressed their reluctance to make available the text of the Convention on the Rights of the Child on the grounds that it will create problems of indiscipline. The teachers' attitude and approach may sap students' understanding and commitment to human rights.

Initiatives of NHRC

The Commission has been deeply concerned with the issue of human rights education ever since its inception in 1993. The National Council of Educational Research and Training (NCERT) published with the support of NHRC a *"Source Book" on human rights*. The purpose of the book is to make available to the teachers, students, policy makers and curriculum developers, a selection of major documents on human rights and human rights education in one volume. Owing to the untiring efforts of the Commission, human rights education has been introduced in the university and college system.

The Commission also constituted a task force to look at the teaching of human rights at school level across the country and suggest as to how human rights education could be made more effective at the school level. The module took full count of recent developments in the teaching of human rights.

The existing teacher-pupil ratio of 1:40 in primary schools and 1:35 in upper primary schools has to be maintained. In the long term, the goal should be a ratio of 1. India's demographic dividend of having a high percentage of young population has to convert to an asset. Educational objectives should be realistic and achievable and there should be a strict time-frame in implementing the right to education.

The NHRC also organized a national level conference on human rights education at school level in New Delhi on March 20, 2009. The objective was to incorporate human rights education in the existing curricula of the school system. The conference recommended that human rights education should be an integral part of the right to education. Inculcation of human rights norms among the students in their formative years will foster among them respect for the dignity of others and help in the building of a tolerant and humane society. It was further recommended that human rights education in schools should be imparted in a child-friendly and child-centric manner. Human rights education through story-telling could be used for primary and middle level school children. As at present, there is no uniformity with regard to imparting human rights education, it was recommended that schools across the country should adopt a common syllabus to facilitate human rights education.

For successful implementation of human rights education in school, it is essential that there should be proper training and education of the teachers so that they can internalize human rights values and convey properly the message of human rights. Training of the teachers should be practical and participatory in nature. The fact that corporal punishment is a gross violation of human rights is to be emphasized before them (during the training). It was further recommended that for effective implementation of human rights education in the school system it is necessary to set up a monitoring committee and building up proper and supportive networks with the parents, civil society groups and the community at large.

In a major effort to set up a centre for excellence for human rights education, the NHRC set up a National Institute of Human Rights at the National Law School of India University, Bangalore in 1999. A chair on Human Rights was also created with the assistance of NHRC.

In order to spread the message of human rights among college and university students, the NHRC conducts internship programmes during summer and winter vacations every year to make the students aware of the working of the Commission as well as other institutions and other international standards relevant to the understanding of human rights. The Commission has also given high priority to the human rights training of the police and security personnel and in consultation with the DGPs worked out a training module for different ranks of the police.

The Commission has helped the NHRIs of Jordan, Nepal, Uganda and Maldives in installing the software for the Complaint Management System as well as the Information System in their local languages. It has signed a MOU with UNDP for capacity building in Afghanistan Independent Human Rights Commission.

The aim of human rights education should be creation of a culture of human rights in the society. For this, it is necessary that citizens are also taught their duties and obligations to society and fellow citizens. In a vast and complex country like India, human rights culture will foster respect for the dignity of others and teach citizens not only their rights but also duties to the state and society. NHRC's human rights training and initiatives have to keep this goal in view.

Note

1. Charles Norchi, Article in Span, September 1995.

12

Review of Laws and International Instruments on Human Rights

The Commission is empowered under sub section (d) and (f) of Section 12 of the Protection of the Human Rights Act, 1993, to study treaties and other international instruments of human rights and make recommendations for their effective implementation. The Commission examines, reviews and gives its independent opinion and views on important Bills and Acts concerning human rights issues. The Commission has till March, 2013 reviewed as many as 16 Acts, Bills or Ordinances including the Child Marriage Restraint Act 1929, Terrorist and Disruptive Activities Act 1985, Prevention of Terrorism Ordinance 2001, Prevention of Torture Bill 2009, Mental Health Care Bill 2011, and the Rights of Persons with Disabilities 2012. The Commission reviewed these Acts and made elaborate comments on their human rights contents.

1. Child Marriage Restraint Act (as given in a previous chapter)
2. Protection of Women from Domestic Violence Act 2005

Domestic violence is a scourge that haunts the country. Despite widespread prevalence, it is not generally acknowledged and has often remained invisible. Very often, acts of violence against the members of the household, whether wife or child, have been perceived as acts of discipline necessary for maintaining the rule of authority in the family.

The Ministry of Women and Child Development drafted a bill on Protection of Women from Domestic Violence that was introduced in Parliament in 2002. It was referred to the standing committee of Parliament for further scrutiny and examination. After receiving the report of the standing committee, the Ministry of Women and Child Development sent a copy of the draft bill along with a copy of the report of the Standing Committee to the Commission for comments. Many of the recommendations of the Commission on the draft bill were subsequently incorporated in the Act. Some of the important recommendations of the Commission that have been incorporated in the Act are as follows:

(a) The Act protects the right of women to secure housing and also a right to reside in the matrimonial home or household.

(b) It provides for appointment of protection officers and registration of non-government organizations as service providers for providing various types of assistance to the aggrieved persons.

(c) The definition of child has been elaborated to include the rights and interests of the children, who have been adopted or are step or foster children.

(d) A new section relating to matters of jurisdiction has been incorporated.

(e) Though the Government of India recommended that the magistrates at any stage of proceedings under the Act may direct the respondent or the aggrieved persons to undergo mandatory counselling with any service provider, the Commission suggested that counselling should be left open to the victim as well as the respondent and this has been agreed to.

The Terrorist and Disruptive Activities Prevention Act 1987.

The Commission conducted a full-fledged examination of all aspects of the Terrorist and Disruptive Activities Prevention Act and also reports and complaints regarding arbitrary and abusive uses of the Act, which flooded the Commission. The Commission, thereafter, followed a three-fold strategy. It continued to closely monitor the manner in which the Act was implemented. It collected data concerning the abuses and misuses of the Act and then when the date neared the consideration of the extension of the life of the statute it made a direct approach to all members of Parliament seeking an end to this law. The Chairman of the Commission sent a letter to all Parliamentarians (dated February 20, 1995) recommending that the Act need not be renewed when its life expired on May 23, 1995 on the grounds that it was "incompatible with our cultural traditions, legal history and treaty obligation[1]". It was a matter of great satisfaction to the Commission and to countless human rights activists in the country that the Act was not revived when its life expired on May 23, 1995.

The Commission also forcefully opposed its resurrection in the form of the Prevention of Terrorism Ordinance 2001. In its opinion, the National Human Rights Commission dwelt extensively on different provisions of the Prevention of Terrorism Bill as proposed by the Law Commission in its 173rd Report. It clearly stated that "Undoubtedly, national security is of paramount importance. Without protecting the safety and security of the nation, individual rights cannot be protected. However, the worth of a nation is the worth of the individual constituting it. Article 21, which guarantees a life with dignity, is non-derogable. Both national integrity as well as individual dignity are core values in the Constitution, and are compatible and not inconsistent. The need is to balance the two. Any law for combating terrorism should be consistent with the Constitution, the relevant international instruments and treaties, and respect the principles of necessity and proportionality. The National Human Rights Commission, therefore, reiterates its earlier view in respect of the Ordinance also".

The Ordinance (4 of 2003) was replaced by the Prevention of Terrorism Act (POTA) 2003; the Commission, however maintained its firm view that a proper balance between the need and the remedy requires respect for the principles of necessity and proportionality. While it is necessary to combat terrorism, counter-terrorism should not be used as an excuse to suspend all the rules of the international law and domestic civil liberties. While combating terrorism, promotion and protection of human rights has always to be kept in view[2].

3. Armed Forces Special Powers Act

Human Rights activists and civil society groups have denounced the Armed Forces Special Powers Act (AFSPA) and held that it has been abused and misused by the security forces. According to them, AFSPA has facilitated extra judicial killing, torture, rape and disappearance which in turn have fed public anger and disillusionment against the Indian state. Officers of the armed forces on the other hand, are of the clear view that diluting special powers of the security forces under the Act will be counter-productive. In order to function effectively, security forces need legal provisions enabling them to conduct proactive operations. Without such laws armed forces in hostile areas cannot function.

The National Human Rights Commission got itself impleaded in the proceedings pending before the Supreme Court and to assist the court by placing the Commission's views before it on the issue that has arisen in that connection. The Commission has held a frank and free discussion (May 13, 1997) with all stakeholders, including, senior most officers of the armed forces, Secretaries of Defence and Home Ministries and others, including, leading academics and representatives of non-government organizations. The views of the Commission were placed before the Supreme Court and the Commission adopted a position that the Act lacked temporal and spatial limitations and could be exercised by junior officers on the basis of the subjective satisfaction[3].

The Supreme Court held that enactment was constitutionally valid. Though the Act may be harsh, on the face of it, it was a necessity. The Apex court also concluded that a declaration under Section 3 of the Act has to be for a limited period and subject to periodic review before the expiry of six months and a person arrested under Section 4 (c) of SPA should be handed over to the officer in charge of the nearest police station so that he can be produced before the nearest magistrate within 24 hours of such an arrest.

The Act remains on the statute despite the recommendation of the Jivan Reddy Committee to withdraw this instrument of intimidation and repression from the North East. The Commission should have taken notice of widespread public outcry against this Act. Time has perhaps come for the union government to take a clear decision without dithering. The Commission perhaps should have held a wider public consultation and taken a clear stand on the continuance of the Act. Recently, the former Home Minister P. Chidambaram has said, "the government has not able to concede the people's demand because the army is not willing to accept even a partial withdrawal of AFSPA, which they hold operationally essential for their working in the disturbed areas".

Freedom of Information Bill 2000

The Commission has taken up the Freedom of Information Bill 2000 for in-depth examination. It also had extensive discussions with NGOs and senior lawyers regarding the contents of the Bill. The Commission took the view that the title of the Bill should be changed from "Freedom of Information Bill" to "Right to Information Bill." The preamble of the Bill, the Commission found, proceeds on the basis that the bill confers for the first time the freedom to access information. The Commission was of the view that the preamble should convey an access to a right which already exists. According to the Commission, it has been judicially recognized that the right to freedom of speech and expression in Article 19 (i) (a) includes the right to acquire information. It is obligatory on the part of the state not only to respect the fundamental rights guaranteed under Part II of the Constitution but also to operationalize the meaningful exercise of these rights. The Supreme Court in the case of Reliance vs Indian Express (1988) 4SCC 592 said, "Right to know is a basic right which citizens of a free country aspire to in the broader horizon of the right to live in this age in our land under Article 21 of our Constitution." The Commission's opinion was confined to the salient features of the Bill as it felt that consideration of details should be undertaken in the light of the basic premise indicated above.

Amendment of the Protection of Human Rights Act, 1973

(Details in the previous chapter)

Food Safety and Standard Bill 2005

The Commission expressed its concern regarding the reported repeal of Infant Milk Substitute (IMS), Feeding Bottle and Infant Foods Act (IMS Act).

As proposed by its inclusion in Schedule I of the Food Safety and Standard Bill 2005, the Chairman of the Commission, in his letter dated March 15, 2005, to the Minister of State, Ministry of Food Processing Industries, conveyed the concern of the Commission in this regard. The Commission pointed out that the IMS Act is not a food law but a special Act to protect, promote and support breast feeding and focus on practices that interfere with breast feeding and jeopardize the health of the baby and the mother. In response, the Ministry of Food Processing Industries informed the Commission that the Group of Ministers has decided that the IMS Act would not be repealed but only amended suitably.

Review of International Conventions

Under Section 12A of the Protection of Human Rights Act, the Commission has statutory responsibility to study treaties and other international instruments on human rights and make recommendations for their effective implementation.

Convention against Torture

Convention against Torture and other Cruel, Inhuman or Degrading Treatment or Punishment was adopted by the United Nations General Assembly on December 10, 1984, (Resolution 39/46). It went into force in June 1987. Torture is rightly considered as the most heinous violation of human rights as it constitutes the denial of the essence of human rights, namely, recognition that each living being has a personality of his own which has to be respected. Torture takes many forms and courses in widely divergent situations. No country, whatever its political system or ideological colour, is indeed free from this scar.

The Convention requires state parties to take adequate and effective steps to prevent torture in any territory under their jurisdiction. Each state party shall ensure that all acts of torture become offences under its criminal law and shall make these offences punishable by appropriate penalties which take into account their grave nature (Article 4). No exceptional circumstances, such as war or public emergency, can be invoked to justify torture (Article 2). Obedience to order from a superior authority or public servant will not be accepted as a justification for torture. Article 14 of the Convention provides that the victim of an act of torture obtains redress and has an enforceable right to fair and adequate compensation. Other forms of cruel, inhuman or degrading punishment as defined in the Convention which may be committed by persons acting in an official capacity are also prohibited. The 1984 Convention not only prohibits torture but also forbids inhuman action on a less macroscopic scale—cruel, inhuman, degrading treatment or punishment.

NHRC played an important role in persuading the Government of India to sign the Convention against Torture. The Commission had to do powerful advocacy at the level of the Prime Minister. But ratification of the Convention unfortunately is still pending. Failure to ratify the Convention has even affected the capacity of the country to secure extradition of persons wanted by law enforcement agencies of India. The Commission has repeatedly pointed out that the prohibition of torture is part of the domestic law of the country, and, therefore, its ratification should not be delayed.

The government has now initiated the procedure of ratification by bringing an Anti-Torture Bill in Parliament which is still pending. The Anti-Torture Bill was introduced by the government in Parliament in 2009. The Bill with many flaws and deficiencies from the human rights angle was passed by the Lok Sabha. Widespread criticism of the draft bill by the human rights activists and jurists stalled its passage in the Rajya Sabha resulting in its reference to the select committee. The Commission is pursuing the passage of the Bill as an essential step towards-much-awaited ratification of the Convention.

UN Convention on Disability

The Commission had advocated to the Government of India for ratification of the optional protocol to the UN Convention on the Rights of Persons with Disabilities. The Commission holds the view that the optional protocol will provide an important tool for promotion of rights of persons with disability and also strengthen the accountability mechanism.

Optional Protocol to the Convention on the Rights of the Child

The Commission strongly recommended to the Government of India that it should ratify the Optional Protocol I and II to the Convention on the Rights of the Child dealing with involvement of children in the armed conflicts and the sale of children, child prostitution and pornography. The Government of India has ratified both the optional protocols. The Optional Protocol to the Convention on the Rights of the Child on the Involvement of Children in

Armed Conflict was ratified on November 30, 2005 with the following Declaration:

"Pursuant to Article 3(2) of the Optional Protocol to the Convention on the Rights of the Child on the involvement of children in armed conflict, the Government of the Republic of India declares that:

(i) The minimum age for recruitment of prospective recruits into Armed Forces of India (Army, Air Force and Navy) is 16 years. After enrolment and requisite training period, the attested Armed Forces personnel is sent to the operational area only after he attains 18 years of age.

(ii) The recruitment into the Armed Forces of India is purely voluntary and conducted through open rally system/open competitive examinations. There is no forced or coerced recruitment into the Armed Forces."

The Optional Protocol to the Convention on the Rights of the Child on the Sale of Children, Child Prostitution and Child Pornography was ratified by the Government of India on August 16, 2005.

Notes

1. Annual Report of the Commission 1994-95.
2. Annual Report of the Commission 2003-04, pp. 50-51.
3. Annual Report of the Commission 1997-98, p. 21.

13
Vulnerable Groups

Elderly Persons

There is a gradual rise in the population of elderly persons in India. From 19.8 million in 1951, it has shot up to 76 million in 2001. It is estimated that the number and above 60 in India will increase to 100 million in 2013 and 190 million in 2030. Along with the increase in the number of elderly persons, there is a corresponding increase in various forms of abuse and violence against them. The International Network for Prevention of Elder Abuse (INPEA) defines elderly abuse as "*neglect and violation of human, legal and medical rights and deprivation of the elderly*" (NHRC Annual Report 2010-11, p. 114). The nature of violence perpetrated against them is not only physical but also mental.

Today, the breakdown of the joint family system is making the lives of elderly people very difficult and lonely. They are often left alone to fend for themselves and no one witnesses violation of their basic human rights. Many of them become soft targets of criminals. Again, because of their inability to live on their own they are forced to employ domestic help without verifying their antecedents. This makes them vulnerable to attacks by criminals and other confidence tricksters. There are a number of cases, particularly in Delhi, of domestic servants employed involved in crimes against their employers. Further, because of failing health the elderly can be easily be over-powered. Many elderly people try to solve the problem by reducing exposure to potentially threatening situations. Because of crimes or fear of crime they do not venture out and develop a fortress mentality. Again, many elderly people are ill-treated by their family members. A recent study by Help Age, a Delhi based non-governmental organization, has revealed that many elderly people are ill-treated by their own children, who have emerged as the largest group of perpetrators.

Human rights are universal and indivisible. Human rights of the elderly are explicitly set out in the Universal Declaration of Human Rights and the International Covenants on Civil and Political Rights and Economic Social and Cultural Rights, Convention on all forms of Discrimination Against Women and other international treaties and declarations.

The following human rights of the elderly should be taken note of as indivisible, interdependent and interrelated.

- The human right to an adequate standard of living, including adequate food, shelter and clothing.
- The human right to adequate social security, assistance, and protection.
- The human right to the highest possible standard of health.
- The human right to be treated with dignity.
- The human right to full and active participation in all aspects of political, economic, social and cultural life of the society.
- The human right to full and effective participation in decision-making concerning their well-being.

The National Human Rights Commission has kept close touch with groups involved in protection of the rights of the elderly and has been transmitting to the central and state government concrete suggestions for protection and promotion of their human rights as and when necessary.

The Commission also constituted a core group on elderly people in November 2010 comprising well-known activists, gerontologists and experts. At a national seminar held in Dehradun on January 20, 2011, by NHRC in collaboration with Anugraha, a Delhi-based NGO, a large number of senior citizens, eminent persons and student volunteers participated.

Miloon Kothari, coordinator Housing and Land Rights Network, South East Asia Regional Programme drew attention of the committee in a petition to the crises of homelessness in Delhi. The Commission called for a report from Delhi administration and was informed that a survey work done by the Institute of Human Development revealed that there were 46,788 shelterless persons in Delhi, of whom 84.35% were men and 15.65% were women and 3% were children. Most of these people were subjected to harassment by the police. The Commission sent the survey report to the Government of NCT Delhi. It was reported by the Delhi government that it had set up a special empowered committee under the chairmanship of the secretary for preparation of an action plan for the benefit of shelterless persons.

There is room for improving security of elderly citizens and India can learn from good practices in other countries. Elderly people in Japan have been singled out for special outreach by the police. They observe "*Silver Days*" when policemen drop in at the homes of the elderly. Particular efforts are also made by the Japanese police to draw them into crime prevention organizations. Sometimes, law enforcement officers who contact senior citizens are young and have little experience of working with the elderly. In the USA, some police departments created special positions called law enforcement gerontologists. They deal with crime and abuse-related problems with the elderly. By developing a rapport with the elderly, the officers identify their problems and then recommend ways to minimize the risks.

It is aptly said that a society is to be judged by how well it protects its children and the elderly. Neglect of elderly people's concerns, including, their fear of crime contributes to the belief that they are being seen as disposable and obsolete. The fear of crime visible in the eyes of the elderly today serves as mirror of our own future.

Manual Scavengers

Manual scavenging refers to removal of human excreta (night soil) from insanitary dry toilets. Dry toilets means, toilets without the modern flush system. The degrading practice of manual scavenging is a severe violation of human dignity and an infringement of human rights of those engaged in the task. It assails the core of human dignity which is the very corner stone of human rights. The right to be free from manual scavenging is an economic, social and cultural right and it imposes an obligation on the state to abolish the manual scavenging system and give relief and rehabilitation to the manual scavengers and their dependents by adopting suitable initiatives.

Though a national scheme was launched in 1992, to liberate those, who are engaged in this demeaning practice the implementation of the scheme has been appallingly poor except in some states. In its Annual Report of 1998-99 the NHRC observes "this speaks of apathy bordering on the unforgivable in respect of a deep societal wrong".

Manual scavenging is also a caste-based hereditary occupation of the Dalits. The International Dalit Solidarity

Network reports that it is estimated that "around 1.3 million Dalits in India, mostly women, make their living through manual scavenging which involves removal of human excrement from dry toilets and sewers. Dalit scavengers are rarely able to take up another occupation due to discrimination related to their caste and occupational status and thus forced to remain scavengers. They are paid less than minimum wages and are often forced to borrow money from upper caste neighbours in order to survive and consequently they "end up maintaining the relationship of bondage".

Men, women and children particularly from Chuhar, Mehathar, Halalkhor, Lalbaghi, Bangi, Thotti and Jamadar lower castes are commonly employed as manual scavengers in India. These caste subgroups are generally referred to as Valmiki in India. The Valmiki is considered to be the lowest among the lowest in the caste hierarchy. Upper caste Hindus considered the Dalits as being untouchables. The Dalits employed as manual scavengers are considered to be untouchables even by other Dalits.

The International Dalit Solidarity Network estimates that around 1.3 million Dalits in India, mostly women, are involved in manual scavenging. It links the job to "forced labour" or "forced slavery" stating that the Dalits are rarely able to take up another occupation due to caste -based discrimination and debt bondage.[1]

Since 1949, several Committees and Commissions had been set up by the government to study manual scavenging and to recommend to the government measures to end manual scavenging. The Barve Committee of 1949, the Scavenging Commission Enquiry Committee of 1957, the National Commission for Labour Committee 1968, and the Commission for Safai Karmacharis have all recommended to the government various means to end manual scavenging in India but very little progress took place on the ground to implement those recommendations.

The Indian Railways, the largest rail network in the world, employs the largest number of manual scavengers. Unofficial surveys by various non-governmental organizations and research groups project that about 12,00,000 persons are employed as manual scavengers in India. The surveys also project that among the manual scavengers 98 per cent are Dalits of which 95 per cent are females.[2]

Legislation

Sanitation is a state subject, but Article 252 of the Constitution empowers Parliament to legislate for two or more states by consent and adoption of such legislation by any other state. After six states passed a resolution requesting the central government to frame a law, the Employment of Manual Scavengers and Construction of Dry Latrine (Prohibition) Act, 1993 drafted by the Ministry of Urban Development was passed by Parliament in 1993. Over time, the Act was enacted by 23 states and Union Territories. Two other states have passed their own laws which are similar. The Act provides penalty of imprisonment up to one year with or without a fine which may extend up to Rs. 2,000 or both in case of failure or contravention of the Act. Further, in case of repeated contraventions, a fine to the extent of Rs. 100 per day for the entire period of contravention is also provided. The 1993 law saw no conviction into its 20 years history, despite widespread prevalence of the practice.[3]

It took about four years for the central government to even notify the law in the Government Gazette. In reality, not all the states have implemented this law. According to a study conducted by Safai Karmachari Andolan about

33 per cent of Indians still use dry latrines. Another 33 per cent of the population do not have toilets in their houses and find it convenient to defecate in open spaces.

The Planning Commission formulated the National Action Plan for total eradication of manual scavenging by 2007. The salient features of the plan were: (1) Identification of manual scavengers (2) The Manual Scavengers and Construction of Dry Latrines (Prohibition) Act 1993 should be adopted by all states where manual scavenging exists. (3) Involvement of Non-Governmental Organizations (NGOs) (4) Ministry of Finance should issue necessary instructions to the nationalized banks (5) Incentives for implementation.

NHRCs Interventions

The National Human Rights Commission and National Commission for Safai Karamcharis have combined their efforts to eliminate the degrading practice of manual scavenging. In coordination with the National Commission for Safai Karamcharis, the Commission organized a joint meeting on April 6, 1999 to chalk out a joint strategy to end this inhuman and degrading practice. It set up a high powered group to pursue the matter and make appropriate recommendations to ensure that plans and programmes to end this practice yield results within a reasonable time frame. In a communication to the Chief Ministers of all states (dated August 14, 2001) the Chairperson of NHRC urged them to ensure replacement of all dry latrines by power flush latrine and totally ban construction of any dwelling house or building, which does not have power flash latrines. He also separately addressed the Prime Minister on this issue. Unfortunately, the response received from the different states was poor and reflected a dismal picture of the Act's implementation.

It also organized a national workshop on Manual Scavenging and Sanitation in New Delhi on August 28, 2008. Some of the important recommendations made by the Commission after the workshop were:

1. The definition of manual scavengers is different from sanitary workers and all authorities must restrict themselves to the definition of manual scavenging as given in the Employment of Manual Scavengers and Construction of Dry Latrines (Prohibition) Act, 1993.
2. The issue of lack of space and scarcity of water in some states have to be addressed by adopting appropriate technology and methodologies.
3. There should be a time-bound limit for conversion of dry latrines to wet latrines and construction of new latrines. It should be one of the criteria for deciding grants to municipal bodies and there should be some measures to take penal action against municipalities not fulfilling their obligations in this regard.
4. The State Human Rights Commissions should start monitoring elimination of manual scavenging and consequent rehabilitation of manual scavengers in the states. At this conference, the Chairman of the National Human Rights Commission said that manual scavenging is an issue of national shame and should be equated with bonded labour and scavengers need to be rehabilitated in a similar manner. SHRCs should have an equal role to play in elimination of the role of manual scavenging.

The National Human Rights Commission also organized a national workshop on manual scavenging and sanitation on March 11, 2011. Some of the important recommendations of the workshop were the following:

1. The employment of Manual Scavengers and Construction of Dry Latrines Prohibition Act 1993 should be implemented in letter and spirit and at a faster pace. The abolition of the practice of scavenging should be taken as a national mission.
2. Till date, there is no single window to address the problems of manual scavengers. A single window should be created in every district with a nodal officer to facilitate and fast track the process of implementation.
3. Cleaning of septic tanks should be mechanized to abolish manual cleaning. Necessary technology has to be adopted.
4. Railway should develop state-of-art technology of sanitation facilities to minimize manual interventions within a fixed time frame.
5. In the case of death or disability, the dependents of the safai karamcharis should be provided with immediate employment in accordance with their qualifications.
6. The rehabilitated manual scavengers should be issued with a BPL card along with scholarship to the children and pension to the widow of the manual scavengers. The existing scheme of rehabilitation of manual scavengers should be revised in order to make it more practical and viable.
7. There have been instances, wherein those appointed for the cleaning task has sublet the task to the erstwhile manual scavengers or some safai karamcharis. The exploitation continues, albeit, indirectly. This trend has to be discouraged and those responsible for doing so have to be given stringent punishment.

Manual scavenging still survives in many parts of India without a proper sewage system. It is considered to be most prevalent in Gujarat, Madhya Pradesh, Uttar Pradesh and Rajasthan. Some municipalities in India still run dry toilets. The biggest violator of this law in India is the Indian railways which has toilet dropping excreta from the trains on the tracks and scavengers are employed to clean it manually[4].

In the national workshop on March 11, 2011, the Chairperson of the National Commission for Scheduled Castes, P.L. Punia mentioned that in UP only 23 per cent of the safai karamcharis are SC and ST. The rest of them are from other categories. But these workers never use the broom as they sublet the work to SC an ST workers. The exploitation thus continues. Even though 18 years have passed after the Act of 1993, the problem still persists. The NGOs and state administration may have different opinions of the number of manual scavengers but this does not dilute the fact that the practice still exists. Recently, the Government of India has passed a new legislation in September 2011, and issued government notification for the same. In December 2011 the government has also formulated rules known as Prohibition of Employment as Manual Scavengers and their Rehabilitation Rules 2013 or MS Rules 2013. The Act prohibits manual scavenging and manual cleaning of septic tanks and sewers. The Act also prohibits unsanitary toilets and will offer assistance in the form of loans and one time grants to former manual scavengers to aid in their search for alternate employment.

Conclusion

It is unfortunate that despite persistent efforts the Commission could not make much headway to achieve elimination of manual scavenging. Manual scavenging continues in different parts of the country as one of the most egregious violations of human rights. The Parliament has now passed the Prohibition of Employment as Manual Scavengers and Their Rehabilitation Bill 2012. The new law has a wider scope for higher penalties than provided under the 1993 Act. Offences under the Act have become cognizable, non-bailable and may be tried summarily. It expands the definition of manual scavenging to bring cleaners of drains, sewers and safety tanks in its ambit. It provides for mandatory rehabilitation of released manual scavengers. The dehumanizing practice of manual scavenging is inconsistent and incompatible with basic human dignity and state authorities as well as human rights institutions have to wage an unflagging struggle to eliminate this monstrous wrong prevalent in the Indian society.

Human Rights Defenders

Defenders of Faith

Human Rights Defenders is a term used to describe people, who individually or with others seek to promote and protect human rights and fundamental freedoms. Though, the primary responsibility for the promotion and protection of human rights rests with the state, the brave human rights defenders play an important role in ensuring that people enjoy human rights without fear. Human Rights Defenders (HRDs) are active in every part of the world in both developing as well as developed countries and they seek to promote and protect human rights in the context of a variety of challenges.

Declaration of HRDs

The adoption of "Declaration on the Rights and Responsibilities of Individuals, Groups and Organs of Society to Protect and Promote Universally Recognized

Human Rights and Fundamental Freedoms" commonly known as "Declaration on HRDs) was adopted by the UN General Assembly in 1998 on the occasion of the 50th Anniversary of the Universal Declaration of Human Rights. The Declaration is addressed not just to the states and Human Rights Defenders but to everyone. It emphasizes that there is a great role for everyone to fulfil as human rights defenders. It also underscores and stresses that there is a global human rights movement which embraces all of us.

Human Rights Defenders are indeed on the front line of the struggle for human rights. They often take up cudgels on behalf of the people against the powers of the state. They address any human rights concern, which can be as varied as summary execution, arbitrary torture and detention, discrimination, access to health care, toxic waste and other environmental issues. In all states, be they democratic or authoritarian, civil society groups are necessary to fight for human rights and to ensure that the states protect human rights and function within the four corners of law and do not overrule them.

A large portion of the activities of the HRDs are devoted to helping victims of human rights violations. Investigation and reporting of violations can act as checks on the perpetrators and assist victims in taking their cases to the courts. Some HRDs provide professional, legal advice and assist victims in taking their cases to the courts. Some even help the victims in the judicial process.

Many of the HRDs often pay a heavy price for their courage of convictions and commitment and encounter various forms of harassment and privations. They themselves become victims of arbitrary arrest, torture or even death.

The Declaration on HRDs is not a legally binding instrument. However, it contains several rights and principles grounded on international human rights standards and enshrined in legally binding international instruments like the International Covenant on Civil and Political Rights. Indeed, the adoption of the Declaration was the culmination of long years of negotiation and lobbying by human rights organizations to ensure international recognition of the crucial role played by HRDs for the promotion and protection of human rights. The Declaration spells out the specific rights and protections accorded to the human rights defenders.

Article 2 specifies that each state has a prime responsibility and duty to protect, promote and implement fundamental freedoms and shall adopt legislative, administrative and other steps as may be necessary to ensure that rights and freedoms referred to in the present Declaration are guaranteed. Article 5 lays down that for promoting and protecting human rights everyone has the right to meet or assemble peacefully and participate in non-government associations or groups and communicate with them. Article 10 prescribes that none shall participate by act or failure to act where required in violating human rights and fundamental freedoms and none shall be subjected to punishment or adverse reaction of any kind for refusing to do so. Article 13 affirms that everyone has the right individually and in association with others to solicit, receive and to use resources for the express purpose of promoting and protecting human rights and fundamental freedoms through peaceful means in accordance with Article 3 of the present Declaration.

Duties of the State

Articles 2, 9, 12, 14 and 15 of the Declaration make particular references to the role of the state and its responsibilities and duties. These are (a) adopt legislative administrative and other steps that may be necessary to ensure effective implementation of rights and freedoms referred to in the present Declaration (b) Provide an effective remedy to persons who claim to have been victims of human rights violations. (c) To ensure that domestic laws are consistent with the UN Charter and other international obligations of the state in the field of human rights and fundamental freedoms. (d) To ensure support for the creation and development of independent national institutions for the promotion and protection of human rights such as Ombudsman or Human Rights Commissions. (e) To promote and facilitate the teaching of human rights at all levels of formal education and professional training. (f) To provide an effective remedy for persons, who claim to have been victims of human rights violations.

Article 5 (b) of Human Rights Defender Declaration says that for the purpose of promoting and protecting human rights and fundamental freedoms everyone has the right individually and in association with others at national and international levels to form, join and participate in non-governmental associations or groups.

No qualification is required to be a human rights defender and the Declaration of HRD makes it clear that we can all be defenders of human rights. Human rights defenders can be of any country, any age and from different backgrounds. It is important to know that HRDs are found not only in NGOs or intergovernmental organizations but in some instances may be civil servants and members of the private sector. Many people working in a professional capacity as human rights defenders are paid a salary for their work but there are many others who receive no remuneration. Many human rights organizations lack adequate financial resources and HRDs acting as volunteers play an invaluable role. Though journalists are not human rights defenders but many journalists function as HRDs when they report or bring to light egregious violations of human rights. Doctors and medical professionals who treat and rehabilitate victims of human rights violations can be termed as human rights defenders in the true sense of the term.

NHRC and HRDs

NHRC has set up a Focal Point to deal with complaints of harassment of HRDs. It ensures that directions of the Commission in cases of harassment of HRDs are complied by authorities concerned and communicated to it and to the victims.

In a workshop organized by the NHRC on Difficulties Faced by Human Rights Defenders on October 12, 2009, difficulties faced by human rights defenders were discussed and a number of appropriate remedial measures were suggested. One of the recommendations was that there is a need to draw a line of distinction between human rights defenders and those who wear the garb of human rights defenders to gain advantages. The human rights defenders have also duties towards the society and in carrying out their activities they should act in a peaceful manner and should not take law into their hands. Complaints of harassments by human rights defenders could be posted on the website to draw people's specific attention to sue cases.

The Commission has visited remote areas of the country to understand the difficulties of the HRDs at the grass root level and sought to rectify the hurdles through the concerned state governments. Complaints received in the Commission have been accorded high priority.

Following the adoption of the Declaration, a number of initiatives have been taken both at international, national and at regional level to strengthen the protection of the Defenders and contribute to the proper implementation of the Declaration. The following mechanisms were established in the context:

1. The Mandate of UN Special Rapporteur of Human Rights Defenders 2000.
2. The Mandate of Special Rapporteur of African Commission on Human Rights Defenders.
3. Human Rights Defender Unit of the Inter-American Commission on Human Rights 2001.
4. European Union Guidelines on Human Rights Defenders 2001.

In March 2008, the Human Rights Council appointed Mrs. Margaret Sokaggya as a special Rapporteur on Human Rights Defenders. She is a Magistrate from Uganda and Chairperson of the Ugandan Human Rights Commission. She succeeded Hena Jilani as the special representative of the Secretary General on the situation of the human rights defenders.

Steps Taken by NHRC for Protection of HRDs

The Human Rights Council of UN in a resolution dated March 15, 2013, urged "States to create a safe and enabling environment in which human rights defenders can operate free from hindrance and insecurity, in the whole country and in all sectors of society, including, by extending support to local human rights defenders". The Council also called upon states to ensure that measures to combat terrorism and preserve national security "are in compliance with their obligations under international law, in particular under international human rights law, and do not hinder the work and safety of individuals, groups and organs of society engaged in promoting and defending human rights".

NHRC has taken some proactive steps to protect the cause of HRDs by recommending prosecution of violators of human rights defenders and compensation to the HRDs. It has organized workshops attended by state functionaries to spread awareness of the role and plight of the human rights defenders. The Commission has taken cognizance of a number of cases of harassment and persecution of human rights defenders. In most of the cases, the Commission has asked for further investigation and submission of reports. However, in most of the cases, as the annual reports of NHRC show that reports from the state authorities are awaited. In one case regarding arrest of five HRDs by the police on allegedly false grounds in Tamil Nadu, the NHRC deputed its own investigation team for spot investigation. The team came to the conclusion that the allegations were true. In this case a CID enquiry had been ordered by the Government of Tamil Nadu.

Justice Rangnath Misra, former Chairperson of NHRC and a member of Parliament referred a complaint of harassment and misbehaviour caused to Usha Kiran Vajpayee, while on duty under the Pulse Polio Programme by the police staff of PS Dakor, District Jalaun, Uttar Pradesh, resulting in amputation of one of her legs. The Commission called for a report from the Government of Uttar Pradesh. The report of the UP Government stated that a charge-sheet has been filed against the delinquent police officials. On consideration of the report, the Commission found that injury resulting in amputation of one of the legs of the victim requires grant of immediate relief u/s 18(3) of the Act and accordingly, issued show cause notice to the Government of Uttar Pradesh. As no reply was received from the UP Government, the Commission awarded Rs. 5 lakhs as interim relief to the victim Usha Kiran Vajpayee to be paid by the government of Uttar Pradesh. In response, the government of Uttar Pradesh informed that a charge sheet had been filed against the delinquent police officials. The state government stated that award of immediate relief of Rs. 5 lakhs is excessive and suggested that an amount of Rs. 1 lakh which has been paid to the victim as interim relief be considered reasonable. The Commission rejected the request of the state government to reduce the amount and reiterated its earlier instructions. The state government agreed to pay the balance amount of Rs. 4 lakhs to the complainant.

The National Human Rights Commission organized a workshop on Human Rights Defenders on October 12, 2009, in Delhi. The objectives of the workshop were (1) to discuss functions and obligations of the state and human rights defenders in protection and promotion of human rights (2) to share difficulties confronted by human rights defenders and suggest appropriate remedial measures. The workshop made a number of recommendations. The recommendations were:

1. There is need to draw a clear line of distinction between genuine human rights defenders and bogus ones, who masquerade, as human rights defenders to gain personal advantages. The Commission also decided that the HRDs have duties towards the society and must act in a peaceful manner and should not take law into their own hands. The NHRC also decided to write to the Government of India to grant permission to the UN Special Rapporteur on Human Rights Defenders to visit India. The Commission felt that the human rights defenders must also focus attention on victims of human rights violations by the non-state actors.

Today, in India, there is monstrous violation of human rights in many ways and forms. The human rights movement in the country is also passing through a phase of transition. It is now transforming from one primarily concerned with violation of civil and political rights to a movement raising concerns across the broad spectrum of human rights from the right to livelihood and a right to employment to the right to fair trial, freedom of expression, etc. Unfortunately, the country is replete with mutually reinforcing inequalities. More than 300 million of the country's 1.2 billion people live below the poverty line. Economic inequality means unequal access to health, education and justice.

Efforts of human rights defenders to champion these basic human rights of the under-privileged and marginalized sections meet with stubborn resistance from entrenched interests. They are branded as anti-national and harassed in various ways. They encounter criminal cases, violence and motivated campaigns to discredit them. They also face attacks from non-state actors in areas of armed conflict. It is the responsibility of the state authorities to offer them protection and punish the perpetrators of violence. This is also enjoined by Article 12 of the Human Rights Defenders Declaration.

But the HRDs must also have responsibilities to shoulder. They must discharge their duties in a peaceful manner. They should also further educate common citizens about the remedies available to them in case of violation of human rights. In a vast and diverse country like India, the best antidote to violation of human rights is an effective synergy between HRDs, state authorities and human rights institutions.

Persons with Disabilities

There is growing evidence, though estimates vary, that people with disabilities comprise between 4 and 8 per cent of the Indian population. The 2001 census found 21.9 million people with disabilities[5] (2.13 per cent of the population). The approach to people with disabilities for a long time has been built on the model of charity. The disabled were considered incapable of enjoying their rights, despite their other capabilities. And they deserve sympathy and consideration. This approach, however, started changing four decades ago, when the disabled started demanding recognition and protection of their rights. Disability became an important concern in the field of human rights nationally as well as globally. Persons with disabilities (PWD) are those, who suffer from physical, mental or psychological impairment of varying degrees either temporarily or permanently. Their lives are stunted and handicapped due to various social, cultural, economic as well as attitudinal barriers which restrict their capacity and hamper enjoyment of rights on an equal basis.

The Constitution of India envisages a very positive role for the state in respect of its disadvantaged citizens. Article 41 enjoins: "The state shall within the limits of its economic capacity and development make effective provisions for securing the right to work, to education and to public assistance in cases of unemployment, old age, sickness and disablement". But for a long time, the government viewed the problem of the disabled as an individual issue and relied on NGOs to secure basic rights like education and health with persons with disabilities. As a consequence, the entire process of development bypassed people with disabilities.

Judicial Interventions

In the case, Indra Sawhney vs Union of India[6], the apex court examined the legality of reservation in favour of the disabled who are not clearly covered by Article 16 of the Constitution. The Court pointed out that mere declaration of the right would not make unequals equal. It is necessary to take positive measures to equip the disadvantaged and handicapped and bring them to the level of the advantaged.

Article 14 and Article 16(1) would permit such positive measures in favour of the disadvantaged.

In Jagdish Sharan and Others vs Union of India (1980 (2) SCC 768), Justice Krishna Iyer, clarified that equality is not being degraded or neglected if there are special provisions in favour of the disabled with a view to helping them to get over their disablement.

In India, there is landmark legislation, named Persons with Disabilities (Equal Opportunities, Protection of Rights and Full Participation) Act, 1995. The Act aims to protect and promote economic and social rights of people with disabilities. The enforcement mechanisms envisaged in the Act include a Central Coordination Committee at the national level and state coordination committees at the state level. It also includes Chief Commissioner (for persons with disabilities) at the national level and Commissioners at the state level. The Chief Commissioner and the Commissioners are entrusted primarily with the task of monitoring utilization of the funds on disabilities allocated to various government departments. They also must take cognizance of cases of violation of the rights of persons with disabilities.

The NHRC has been deeply concerned and actively involved in the protection and promotion of rights of persons with disabilities and holds the firm view of ensuring that persons with disabilities must enjoy all human rights equally with others. For this, the Commission adopted a multi-pronged approach for the protection and promotion of rights of persons with disabilities. This includes redressal of individual complaints, policy reform, improvement of infrastructure and services as well as research, training and spreading awareness.

As early as in the year 1994-95, the Commission expressed deep concern for the prisoners with mental disabilities and recommended that special arrangements have to be made for looking after mentally sick prisoners in jails. The Mental Health Act of 1987, which replaces the Lunacy Act of 1977, does not permit mentally ill persons to be kept in prisons. The then Chairman of the National Human Rights Commission, Justice Ranganath Mishra as early as on September 11, 1996, in a letter to all the Chief Ministers indicated that mentally ill persons should not be lodged in jails along with other ordinary prisoners. The Commission made it clear that it would detail its officers to inspect as many jails as possible and if any mental patient is found detained in such jails, the NHRC would award compensation to the mental ill persons or to the members of the family and ask the state government to recover the money from the defaulting public officials.

The Commission was also not satisfied with the implementation of Persons with Disability (Equal Opportunities Protection of Right and Full Participation) Act, 1995 and asked for information from the state governments regarding measures taken for job reservation, reservation in admission to various educational institutions, allotment of government quarters for the benefit of disabled persons, etc. It also directed that the Chief Commissioner for persons with disabilities at the central level and the Commissioner for Disabilities at the state level must take energetic steps to deal with various issues related to the implementation of the Act. In a case, regarding a starvation death in Orissa, the Commission recommended provision of disability pension.

The Convention on the Rights of Persons with Disabilities was adopted by the United Nation General Assembly in December, 2006 and opened for signature in March, 2007. The object of the convention is to ensure that persons suffering from disabilities enjoy human rights on an equal basis with others. The Commission played an important role in drafting the Convention on Rights of Persons with Disabilities (CRPD). It also advocated for inserting Article 33 that relates to national implementation and monitoring mechanisms. It strongly urged the Government of India for early ratification of the CRPD and the government ratified the same in October, 2007.

Article 33 of the CRPD deals with national implementation and monitoring mechanisms. It directs the states to constitute one or more focal points within the government for matters relating to implementation of the Convention and establishes a suitable mechanism. As a follow up action the Commission, on its part, appointed a Special Rapporteur on women, children and disability-related issues and constituted a core group consisting of experts and human rights activists. The core group was constituted with the following terms of reference:

- To advise NHRC on maters connected with and incidental to the promotion, protection, and monitoring of rights mentioned in the Indian Constitution; laws for persons with disabilities; and also monitoring rights as envisaged in Article 33(2) of the CRPD.
- To support NHRC in building the capacity of stakeholders, who are strategically important on the rights of persons with disabilities and to monitor recommendations made by NHRC.
- To study the functioning of focal points/coordination mechanisms set up by the centre and states and to suggest improvements for greater effectiveness to the Commission.
- To bring cases of violation of rights of persons with disabilities to the notice of NHRC.
- To advise the Commission on the changes to be brought about in Indian laws and policies in the wake

of India signing and ratifying the CRPD, for onward recommendation to the government.[7]

In the year 2000-01, the Commission sought to plug some loopholes in the Disability Act for better implementation. It enlarged the definition of disability by including persons who experience physical, intellectual and psychological impairments in varying degrees either temporarily or permanently and whose lives are handicapped by social, cultural and attitudinal barriers. The other suggestion covered, inter alia, the composition of central and state coordination committees, reservation in jobs for those with mental retardation and provisions relating to non-discrimination, care and protection. The Commission further took note of non-availability of books in Braille for blind students studying under the state education board. In a letter to all the Chief Ministers of all the states, the Chairman NHRC highlighted the need to ensure printing of books in Braille simultaneously with printing of regular books. The Commission recommended that the State Education Board should take steps to print books in Braille and ensure proper distribution so that such books become available to visually challenged persons and students do not suffer any hardship on that account.

The Commission also reviewed the working draft of Persons with Disability Act, 2011, prepared by the drafting committee constituted by the Ministry of Social Justice and Empowerment. The Committee is seeking to prepare a new law to replace the existing PWD Act, 1995. The Commission has advised the Ministry of Social Justice and Empowerment to ensure that explicit provisions on property rights on persons with disabilities are incorporated in the draft legislation. It has been brought to the notice of the Commission that persons with disabilities incur heavy expenses in terms of assistive devices, transport and other expenses, which causes financial hardship to them. The Commission has recommended to the Union Finance Ministry to make provisions in the Income Tax laws with a view to providing higher exemption limits to persons with disabilities. The Commission also noted that insurance companies are charging extra premium for persons with disabilities in relation to certain health and life insurance policies. The Commission is of the view that such an act of charging extra premium for the persons with disabilities is a violation of Articles 14 and 21 of the Constitution of India and is against the letter and spirit of Articles 25 and 10 of the UN Convention on the Rights of Persons with Disabilities. It advises the government to issue directions to nationalized insurance companies not to charge higher rates of premium from persons suffering from disabilities.

The Commission has intervened effectively in a number of cases of harassment and discrimination on grounds of disabilities and provided relief to the victims. In a landmark case, a medical student, who lost his eyesight during the course of his MBBS studies was enabled to complete his studies and take the final examination, despite unhelpful attitudes of the official agencies, including, the Indian Medical Council.

The Commission has also viewed with concern that in many states, the Commissioner of persons with disabilities holds dual charge as Disability Commissioner as well as the Secretary of the State Department. The Commission has strongly recommended to all states to post a full-fledged Disability Commissioner, without burdening him with other responsibilities.

Effective enjoyment of human rights by people suffering from disabilities is possible only when those responsible for civil administration, maintenance of law and order and the judiciary are adequately sensitized and appreciate the fact that people with disabilities have the same rights as others. In order to help them enjoy these rights special benefits have been provided by special laws, policies and schemes. Not only the people in authorities but society in general must be well aware of these measures, so that they can help people with disabilities to fully enjoy their rights. Hence, it is of vital importance to create wider understanding and appreciation of the human rights of persons suffering from disabilities.

However, in this connection, I feel sorry to mention that the Disability Core Group reconstituted by the Commission in 2009-10 has met only twice in June, 2011, and August, 2011. This perhaps reflects lack of concern which is unacceptable particularly in view of the draft law on disability and mental health care which seeks to bring existing legislation in harmony with UNCRPD. It is also unfortunate that the post of Special Rapporteur on Disability has been lying vacant since December, 2011.[8]

Notes

1. Manual Scavenging (http://idsn.org/caste-discrimination/key-issues/manual-scavenging/) International Dalit Solidarity Network. Retrieved April 8, 2013.
2. "Manual Scavengers: Indian Railways in Denial" (http://southasia.oneworld.net/features/manual-scavenders-indian-railways-n-denial#.UWMxqMrgUoI) One World South Asia. February 25, 2013.
3. "Get Serious" (http://www.thehindu.com/opinion/editorial/get-serious/article5120916.ece). *The Hindu*. September 2013. Retrieved September 16, 2013.
4. "Manual Scavengers Become Fashion Models." (http://news.bbc.co.uk/2/hi/south_asia/7489296.stm BBC. July 4, 2008.
5. NHRC Annual Report 2010-11, p. 117.
6. 1992 Supp (3) SCC.
7. National Human Rights Commission, Annual Report 2007-08, p. 124.
8. National Human Rights Commission, A Retrospective, published in the *Journal National Human Rights Commission in India*, Vol. XII, 2013.

14
Social and Economic Rights

Right to Food

Article 25(1) of the Universal Declaration of Human Rights (UDHR) clearly states that everyone has a right to a "*standard of living, adequate for the health and well-being of himself and family including food, clothing, housing, medical care and necessary social service*". The International Covenant on Economic, Social and Cultural Rights (1966) developed this concept further and laid stress on the "*fundamental right of everyone one to be free from hunger*". India is a state party to ICCPR and has, thus, an obligation to protect and fulfil the right to food for every citizen of India.

The Indian Constitution does not contain any specific provision that recognizes the right to food of every citizen. But Article 21 of the Constitution guarantees the right to life, including, the right to live with dignity and enjoy freedom from hunger. Right to food, is thus, embedded in the right to life enjoined by the Constitution. Further, Article 39(a), a Directive Principle of the Constitution, clearly stipulates that the state must direct its policy to secure an adequate means of livelihood for all its citizens. Article 47, another Directive Principle emphasises the duty of the state to raise the level of nutrition and improve the standard of living of the people. Thus, Article 21 of the

Constitution, when read in conjunction with the Directive Principles, clearly emphasizes the right to food and food security for all citizens.

Despite laudable economic progress during the last two decades, India continues to remain in the category of nations where hunger is *"alarming"*. The Hunger and Malnutrition Report (popularly known as Hangama) released by the Prime Minister in 2013, shows the extent of the malnutrition among children in the rural districts of India. Now, according to the latest report on *State of Food Security in the World* released by the UN Food and Agricultural Organization (FAO), India accounts for the highest number of malnourished children in the world. It is estimated to be 194.6 million; India has thus overtaken China, which has been able to cut its number from 289 million in 1990-92 to 133.8 million. Against this sombre background, the NHRC has strongly advocated the need to ensure the right to food.

A PIL, alleging starvation deaths in Koraput, Kalahandi, and Bolangir districts of Odisha, was filed in the Supreme Court by the Indian Council of Legal Aid and Advice in 1997. The apex court directed the NHRC to study the situation prevailing in these districts and take preventive measures. It authorized the Commission to take legal and enforceable measures for relief and development after ascertaining full facts and assessing the situation. The Commission closely monitored the situation in the districts affected by starvation deaths, held a series of meetings and issued detailed instructions for the relief of the hunger-stricken people in those areas. Along with short-term measures for relief, it recommended long-term plans for sustainable development of the KKB region, to end the chronic cycle of deprivation, malnutrition and starvation. The long-term development plans included sanitation, primary health care, social security measures, relief kitchens, etc. The Commission also held a number of court hearings for this purpose. The Special Rapporteur of the Commission visited the affected areas a number of times and verified the reports submitted by the state government. The matter was closed in 2006, with directions for continued execution of the action plan by the state and monitoring through a system of community surveillance and public audit.

Core Group

The Commission also constituted a core group on right to food, which advises the Commission on all matters having a bearing on right to food and food security. It comprises 18 members. In its meeting on November 2, 2010, the Committee discussed, inter alia, issues like child nutrition, starvation deaths reported from different parts of the country, farmer suicides, sustainable food security, working of the public distribution system, etc.

The Commission had done an evaluation of ICDs in Gorakhpur and found that despite the Supreme Court's order to provide hot cooked meals, all centres supplied packaged meals which contained only 100 calories as against the norm of providing 500 calories. Sixty-three per cent of food and funds were misappropriated. The food is unpalatable and half of it ends up as cattle-feed. Unfortunately, such issues are seldom discussed in state assemblies and Parliament.

It is unfortunate that India has not published comprehensive data on nutrition and health since a national assessment in 2007. However, a country-wide survey involving 2,00,000 interviews were conducted in 2013 and 2014 by UNICEF and the Indian government. Though the full report has not been published, a limited set of data was released by the Ministry of Health. The Report known as

"Rapid Survey on Children" (RSOC) showed some gains both at national and state levels. The report says that a decade ago, 42% of all children were under-weight. Now the reported rate is just below 30%. Madhya Pradesh reduced the number of its children going hungry from 60% to 36% and Bihar from 56% to 37%.

Food Security Bill

The Food Security Bill was passed in Parliament in 2013. It is a landmark legislation which extends to the entire country but comes into force on different dates in different states. The Act promises to provide 5 kgs of food per person per month to *"priority"* households and 35 kgs for *"Antyodaya"* households (called eligible households). The Food Security Bill is an important legislation to fight endemic hunger but its success depends on proper implementation. Service delivery has to be improved and slippage and corruption have to be firmly controlled. Passing of the Act is a necessary but not sufficient condition for reducing hunger.

Food insecurity and hunger often emanate from wrong policies, poor monitoring, bad governance and lack of political will. Economic growth alone will be insufficient to bring about improvement in the situation. Without a major shift in policies and improvement in effectiveness of their implementation, the goal of food security will continue to elude the country.

Right to Health

The right to health is recognized as an important human right in various international instruments. Article 12(1) of the Covenant on Economic, Social and Cultural Rights (ICESCR) affirms that *"the states parties must recognize the right of everyone to the enjoyment of the highest attainable standard of physical and mental health"*. Right to health is recognized in

Article 5(e) of the International Convention of Elimination of All Forms of Racial Discrimination (ICERD). The right to health has also been affirmed in the Vienna Declaration and Programme of Action in 1993 and other international instruments like Declaration and Programme of Action of the Fourth World Conference on Women held in Beijing in 1995. Right to health is closely linked to other human rights like right to food, human dignity, life, non-discrimination, etc. India is a state party to all these Conventions and Declarations. Article 21 of the Indian Constitution embraces the right to health within the rubric of right to life with dignity. Elie Wiesel, the Nobel Prize Laureate, has said, "one cannot, one must not approach public health today without looking for its human rights contents".

The National Human Rights Commission has been seriously concerned with the protection and promotion of the right to health. The Commission's involvement with the right to health started in 1996-97 with identification of maternal anaemia caused by iron and iodine deficiencies as an important human rights issue. In 2000, it constituted a core advisory group on health and organized a workshop on "*Health and Human Rights in India with Special Reference to Maternal Anaemia*". And again in April, 2001, it held a major regional consultation on "*Public Health and Human Rights*" dealing with access to health care and nutrition. It also organized in 2004, five public hearings across the country where problems presented by 1000 persons, belonging to marginalized sections of the society were effectively addressed. This was followed by a national level hearing resulting in the formation of a National Action Plan (NAP), which recommended enactment of a National Public Service Act. A national review meeting on health was organized at the initiative of the Commission in March, 2007, and pursuant to the decision in this meeting the Commission took up various issues like silicosis, endosulfan, flurosis, etc., prenatal sex selection as its special concerns and identified strategies to deal with them. The recommendations, which emerged out of the regional review meetings, have been sent to all stakeholders and are being followed up.

Silicosis

The Commission has been seriously concerned about health hazards posed by silicosis, an occupational disease caused due to inhaling of dust containing free crystalline silica. Crystalline silica or crystalline di-oxide is found in quartz, sandstone, slate and in a number of mineral ores and many common building materials. All those, who are engaged in manufacture of ceramic glass and abrasive powders, are susceptible to silica dust. However, owing to lack of awareness among the doctors, silicosis is often confused with other diseases. The number of people, who die from silicosis is high but exact statistics are not available. It is a disabling and irreversible disease and affects seriously the well-being of the workers and their families.

In 2009, the Commission constituted an expert group under the Chairmanship of one of its members. The expert group identified silicosis-prone industries and suggested preventive remedial and rehabilitative measures. Some of the measures recommended were:

1. Dust control devices should be installed to reduce the dust generation at the workplace. The National Institute of Occupational Health (NIOH) has developed control devices for agate, grinding and quarts crushing industries based on the principle of local exhaust ventilation. The use of wet-drilling and dust extractors may be enforced by respective regulatory authorities.

2. The workers vulnerable to silicosis need to be made aware of the disease through wide publicity campaigns with the use of electronic and print media. This will also improve self-responding of cases and facilitate early detection.
3. It is necessary to develop Master Trainers to impart training to all public health doctors/paramedics for early diagnosis and detection of silicosis.
4. Silicosis control programmes should be integrated with the already existing Revised National Tuberculosis Control Programme (RNTCP).
5. In each of the districts, where a silicosis-prone industry, quarrying or a big construction projects is on, there is the need to identify facilities for diagnosis of silicosis.
6. The accountability for the implementation and control over the rules and regulation of laws must be reviewed from time to time.
7. The National/State Social Security Board set up under the Unorganized Workers' Social Security Act, 2008, should recommend welfare schemes to be formulated for the welfare of the unorganized workers who are at risk of contracting silicosis as well as those already affected and their families.
8. The silica-affected persons should be adequately compensated.
9. The compensation could be calculated based on Disability Adjusted Life Year (DALY) developed by the World Health Organization.

Endosulfan

The Commission had taken cognizance of media reports regarding adverse effects of aerial spraying of endosulfan pesticide on the local population in Kasargod district of

Kerala. It deputed an independent investigation team for enquiry. The report of the investigation team confirmed continued high incidence of medical disorders recorded among people and inadequate relief provided to them by the government of Kerala. The Commission called an urgent meeting of the Core group on health (December 24, 2010) with a view to seeking expert advice on the issue. The core advisory group after studying the available evidence suggested that the Commission should also recommend banning of the use of endosulfan. It was suggested that the Commission should recommend that the state government must provide adequate medical relief to the affected people and pay compensation to them for the health injuries and disorders they suffered. The Commission, later on, made detailed recommendations to the union government and Kerala government. It recommended that the central government must take administrative as well as legislative action to ban the use of Endosulfan and also conducted a nationwide survey of the problem. It recommended that the government of Kerala must pay more compensation to 178 cases of confirmed death in which only Rs. 50,000 each was paid. The need to create greater awareness among the public through a widespread media campaign was also reiterated.

Illustrative Cases

Some of the illustrative cases dealt with the Commission are detailed below:

1. U.K. Sarda, Editor of *Egalitarian Fortnightly,* in his complaint before the Commission, December 24, 2007, invited the attention of the Commission on the death of 13 children in Niloufer Hospital Hyderabad. It was alleged that they had not received proper and adequate treatment due to an unexpected strike of the doctors. The Commission

sought a report from the government of Andhra Pradesh in the matter. The state government informed the Commission that (1) An Enquiry Committee consisting of five senior doctors had been constituted to look into the incident. Their report mentioned that most of the babies were newly born and had extremely low birth weight. These babies also had grave respiratory complications, convulsions and brought in a moribund state from other hospitals. (2) The report stated that there should have been a close and appropriate electronic monitoring of these babies or intensive intervention and support should have been provided depending upon the resources available at that point of time.

The Commission in its order on October 25, 2010, directed the government of Andhra Pradesh to take appropriate steps to deal with such emergencies and improve the overall condition in Neloufer Hospital.

2. In the Annual Report 2010-11, the Commission referred to the death of a patient due to negligence of the staff nurses in Shambunath Pandit Hospital in Kolkata, West Bengal (Case No. 120/25/2006-2007). There was a media report that on November 5, 2005, a female patient was admitted to the Shambunath Hospital for an eye treatment but due to negligence of the hospital authorities, the patient suffered insect bites in her eyes and died. Pursuant to the directions of the Commission, it was reported that the said incident occurred because of the negligence of the six staff nurses and they have been censured. The Commission deprecated the negligence of the hospital authorities leading to the loss of the life of a patient. It held that the state is liable for the negligence of the employees and once death by negligence in the hospital is established, the state is liable to pay damages. It directed the West Bengal government to pay Rs. 100,000 as interim

relief under 18(c) of PHR Act 1993, to the next of the kin of the deceased Gouri Chakraborty. The directions of the Commission were complied with by the state government.

Mental Health

The World Health Day in 2001, proclaimed the theme of mental health and gave the slogan "Stop Exclusion, Dare to Care". In his message, the then UN Secretary General, Kofi Annan said, "mental illness ravages the hidden landscapes of the human mind often with no outward physical signs to betray its debilitating effects. In turn, many who suffer from such disorders suffer in silence, trapped by the shame and stigma of their very often treatable diseases... on this World Health Day, let us commit ourselves to the task to ensure that those who suffer from mental illness no longer suffer in silence".

Human rights of the mentally ill persons have also been a key concern of the Commission. As a part of the mandate given to the Commission by the Supreme Court, it has been monitoring the functioning of the three mental hospitals in Agra, Gwalior and Ranchi. The Supreme Court's order spelt out the contours of this monitoring. The Court's direction was based on the report of a high level committee of the Government of India suggesting the crying need for improvements of diagnostics and therapeutic facilities as well as administration and management of these institutions. The Chairman, Members, special rapporteurs and officers of the Commission have been visiting these institutions and finding out the conditions of the inmates there. The Commission was distressed at the unsatisfactory conditions prevailing in many of the hospitals which were functioning as *"custodial rather than therapeutic institutions"*. Mental health continues to be a deprived area and results in greater deprivation of the already deprived.

In order to tackle the issue in a systematic way, the NHRC entrusted a research project on "*Quality Assurance of Mental Hospitals*" to the National Institute of Mental Health and Neuro Sciences (NIMHANS) Bangalore. The Commission sanctioned to the institute an amount of Rs. 6 lakhs for the project. Based on the report of the NIMHANS in 1999, the Commission has in persuance of the Supreme Court mandate reviewed the working of other mental health institutions. During the year 2010-11, the Commission organized four regional review meetings on mental health in different parts of the country with a view to assessing the prevailing conditions of the mental hospitals and the status of implementation of various mental health programmes. Recommendations emerging out of the review meetings have been sent to all stakeholders and are being followed up.

The Commission's intervention had also resulted in the discharge of a number of persons languishing in mental hospitals for years and quashing of criminal trials against the mentally ill undertrial prisoners. There is a pathetic case of Lallung Morchong, who was released on March 3, 2005, after spending 54 years in Tejpur Mental Hospital, including, 35 years after being declared fit for discharge. This case, which shook the conscience of the nation was widely reported in the print and electronic media. The Commission's monitoring has had the effect of improving the working conditions of the mental institutions of Ranchi, Agra and Gwalior because of its powers to issue legally enforcing decisions as authorized by the Supreme Court. The Commission, however, found that conditions in state mental institutions continue to remain poor because of infrastructural deficiencies and poor management. The NHRC brought the matter to the notice of the Supreme Court through a writ petition filed in 2012. The Supreme Court has now called for replies from central and state governments to a number of specific issues raised in the petition.

Right to health is a basic human right. Basic rights, according to philosopher Henri Shue, are rights that are not only important but also serve as necessary foundations for all other rights. Food, housing and health are basic rights because individuals obviously cannot meaningfully exercise their political rights if they are dying of malnutrition or malaria. Basic rights, according to Shue, include both material subsistence, (economic, social and cultural rights) and physical security (civil and political rights). The state should guarantee these basic rights to everyone to the greatest extent possible.[1]

Today, there are roughly one billion people in the world who lack access to basic material needs. Over 20,000 people die every day from malnutrition or preventable illness. If human rights are to be relevant they must primarily concern basic human needs like access to food, housing and health. Western human rights activists have ignored these rights for decades and this is one of the reasons why many groups of people in the world feel that the International Human Rights Regime is a biased institution that does not address their main concerns.[2]

Food, housing and health care which were long considered as *"step sisters in the field of human rights"* are now gaining more attention from the state, NGOs and international organizations because without them full flowering of human dignity is not possible. Nobel laureate Amartya Sen has named illiteracy, malnutrition and lack of health as the "three unfreedoms" in a democratic country. In a similar vein, Mrs. Mary Robinson, the then UN High Commissioner of Human Rights, in her keynote address at the International Coordinating Committee of National Human Rights Institutions, has aptly observed that "National Human Rights Institutions have the full range of human rights in their remit. An area which has not been touched on is the right to health. Weakness in the delivery of proper health care is a matter of great human rights concern".

Notes

1. Henri Shue, *Basic Rights*. Princeton University Press, 1996, p. 19.
2. Joanne Bauer, "The Challenge to International Human Rights" in *Construction Human Rights in the Age of Globalization*, edited by Mahmood Monshipouri et al., Armonk, NY: Sharpe, 2003.

15
Evaluation

Constitution of the National Human Rights Commission in 1993 marks a milestone in the annals of the human rights movement in the country. A retrospective study shows that that the record of performance of the Commission during the last two decades is somewhat mixed. It has done some laudable and path-breaking work in creating human rights consciousness in the country. It has sensitized and alerted public servants and political authorities over many issues concerning human rights. But in many spheres of human rights promotion and protection, its record is uninspiring and over the years there has been a steady decline of its credibility. Civil society groups have (at times unfairly) become critical of the Commission and the government no longer takes its recommendations seriously. A combination of external and internal factors has been responsible for the failure of the NHRC to play an effective role as a stalwart defender of human rights in the country. The Protection of Human Rights Act (PHRA) gives the Commission only recommendatory powers. It cannot issue judicially enforceable orders giving rise to the criticism that it lacks teeth. Section 19 of the PHRA further emasculates the Commission and prevents it from enquiring into violations of human rights by the armed forces which include within its ambit the para military forces. The Commission, thus cannot enquire into the cases of violation of human rights in the insurgency-affected areas in Kashmir and the North-East by the armed forces.

NHRC has strongly and persistently pressed the state governments for setting up of State Human Rights Commissions (SHRCc) for promoting human tights all over the country. NHRC wanted to have a supervisory role over SHRCs with a view to ensuring that NHRC and the SHRCs act in tandem and not at cross purposes. This would have ensured some uniformity in policy programmes and action. But under the PHRA, each SHRC is an independent entity created by the state government over which NHRC exercises very little supervisory control. Moreover, the Act stipulates that the NHRC cannot enquire into any matter pending before a State Commission and this provision has been used by scheming violators to avoid an inconvenient forum and getting the complaint filed before the forum of their own choice. The need for NHRC's supervision has become all the more important and necessary after the amendment of the PHRA allowing NHRC to transfer in appropriate cases, complaints filed before it to SHRCs. Again over the years, many of the SHRCs have become ineffective and dysfunctional and ceased to command credibility before public eyes.

Complaints

The Commission receives many complaints. Handling of complaints is one of the key indicators of the effective functioning of Human Rights Commissions. Judged by this yardstick, NHRC's record is mixed. The Commission receives several complaints of violation of human rights and the number has swelled exponentially over the years. From the lowly figure of 169 in 1993-94 it shot up to 1,06,990 in 2012-2013. This speaks of the growing credibility of the NHRC and yearning of the people for trouble-free expeditious justice. The Commission has awarded compensation to the victims in numerous cases and has also ensured that its recommendations in this regard, are complied with by the state governments, but it has failed to ensure in many cases that the errant violators are visited with condign punishment. Again, disposal of a large number of cases in limini causes frustration and disappointment amidst the complainants. It is true that many of the complaints do not fall within the remit of the Commission, but unless a very transparent procedure is followed in limini disposal of many complaints will continue to cause frustration and disappointment among the complainants. Reasons for in limini disposal should be clearly indicated and explained to the complainants. It seems that the Commission has become a victim of its own formalism. A more victim-centred, responsive approach should replace a formal and legalistic one. Complaints against the police constitute the bulk of complaints before the Commission. However, the complaints against the armed forces are few and they constitute less than one per cent of the total complaints filed before the Commission. This perhaps is due to the perception in the public mind that the Commission exercises limited control and jurisdiction over the armed forces.

There have been repeated delays on the part of the government in tabling the Annual Reports of the Commission together with the "action taken" report by the government before the Parliament. Such delays are unacceptable as they deny the right to information to the people of the country and unless the reports are placed before Parliament the Commission is not able to release them. The Commission's efforts to amend the PHRA so that the Annual Reports can be released by the Commission if the government delays beyond three months in tabling it before the Parliament have not been successful.

The credibility of the Commission depends to a large extent on public respect and trust for the Chairperson and members of the Commission. The NHRC, during the period of more than twenty years, had some outstanding Chairpersons and members respected for their probity and intellectual acumen. But there were members, who viewed the job as sinecures and took a lukewarm interest in their work. The Ahmadi Committee recommended that the Chairperson of the Commission should be a member of the appointing committee so that his views in the selection of members are taken into consideration. The recommendation was not accepted by the government and thus the Chairperson has no say in the choice of the members. PHRA provides that the Commission will have two members with knowledge of and practical experience in matters relating to human rights. This salutary recommendation was not accepted by the government. Over the years retired IPS or IFS officers have been appointed as members of the Commission as persons with experience in the field of human rights. Appointment of two of the members of the Commission in the past as Governors of states had dented the independent image of the Commission. The NHRC, however has a few laudable achievements to its credit. Despite constraints and infirmities it has played a transformative role in creating human rights consciousness in the country and putting on alert public servants and agencies committing violation of human rights. It has displayed laudable initiative in taking suo moto cognizance of important human rights issues and concerns like police reforms, prison reforms, child labour, bonded labour, custodial deaths, torture, etc. It displayed laudable activism in taking suo motu cognizance of the communal conflagration in Gujarat and exposing the failure of the state government in firmly controlling it. The Commission has brought to the centre stage social, cultural and economic rights of the people. Owing to the Commission's advocacy and insistence, the salience of social and economic rights of the people in evaluating the effectiveness of the Indian state is getting recognized.

The task of enforcing Vishakha guidelines enjoined by the Supreme Court for prevention of sexual harassment of women at workplaces fell on the Commission and it succeeded in setting up complaints committees in different government offices and public sector undertakings and persuading the government to treat such harassment as serious misconduct. Unfortunately, many of these complaint committees have become dysfunctional and the NHRC is in no position to activize them.

In the ultimate analysis, effectiveness and public respect for the Commission depend in a large measure on the competence and credibility of the members of the Commission as well as the political will of the government to support the Commission and make it an effective instrument for protection of human rights. For effective functioning, a Human Rights Commission needs adequate financial and administrative powers, representation of civil society groups in its governing bodies and induction of qualified and sensitized staff.

Admittedly human rights in a developing country like India have a transformative potential. They constitute challenges to the entrenched interests and provide tools for building a just and humane society. The NHRC in its chequered annals of more than two decades have been able to right many wrongs done to individuals and wipe the tears from some eyes. But it has encountered stubborn resistance from entrenched interests as well as from authorities while trying to bring about systemic changes.

Index